SURVIVING THE TECH TSUNAMI

© 2019 by TGS International, a wholly owned subsidiary of Christian Aid Ministries, Berlin, Ohio.

All rights reserved. No part of this book may be used, reproduced, or stored in any retrieval system, in any form or by any means, electronic or mechanical, without written permission from the publisher except for brief quotations embodied in critical articles and reviews.

ISBN: 978-1-949648-65-2

Cover and text layout design: Kristi Yoder

Printed in the USA

Published by:

TGS International
P.O. Box 355
Berlin, Ohio 44610 USA
Phone: 330.893.4828
Fax: 330.893.2305
www.tgsinternational.com

TGS001907

SURVIVING THE TECH TSUNAMI

GARY MILLER

TABLE OF CONTENTS

Part One: Change—The Historical Battle 7
   1. The Tech Tsunami 9
   2. Where Will This Lead? 13
   3. Defining Technology 19
   4. Categorizing Technology 25
   5. Technological Change: Different Perspectives 31
   6. Are All Tools Created Equal? 37

Part Two: Is Something Else Happening Here? 43
   7. Vital Relationships: The Core of Who We Are 45
   8. God and Google 51
   9. Connected and Lonely 59
   10. Media Matters 67
   11. A Sound-Bite Society 73
   12. Brain Change 81

Part Three: Deadly Diversions 89
   13. Digital Distractions 91
   14. Seduced by Sight and Sound 97

15. Entertainment—Changing Our Views and Values 105
16. Pop Culture versus Kingdom Culture 111
17. "Being Bored Is Boring!" 119
18. Circumventing God's Design 127

Part Four: Where Are We? 137
19. The Current Quandary 139
20. Just Say No 147
21. Just Focus on Biblical Principle 155
22. Technology and Our Concept of Church 163
23. The Scourge of Porn 173
24. What Are We Listening To? 179

Part Five: Re-Evaluating Our Course 187
25. Electronic Seduction 189
26. Opportunity of Our Day 195
27. How Should Churches Prepare? 203
28. Higher Ground 211

Endnotes 223
About the Author 230
Additional Resources by Gary Miller 231
Bibliography 235

PART ONE 1

CHANGE—
THE HISTORICAL
BATTLE

CHAPTER ONE

THE TECH TSUNAMI

I purchased my first desktop computer in 1983. Accompanied by a teacher from the local community college, I went to a technology tradeshow and bought a Morrow Designs computer for the small business I wanted to start. It came with an amber screen that blinked "C:" as it awaited my instructions, and two 5 ¼-inch floppy drives that hummed and whirred. Each removable floppy disk could store 200 kilobytes (kb) of data, which seemed like an astounding amount of storage. After all, it takes about 4,800 kb to hold a King James Bible, so with only 24 disks I could hold the entire Bible!

I came home that evening with my professor's assurance that I had the latest in desktop technology. I was also about $2,000 poorer. That seemed like a lot of money, but I was satisfied. I understood that purchasing the latest technology wasn't always cheap.

About a year later our home was broken into and the computer was stolen. To the store I went, only to discover that great progress had been made in computer technology during the past year. This time I returned home with a new computer that had something called a hard drive. Now I no longer had to store my information on floppies. Instead, an incredible little built-in disk (I could hear it whirring inside) could hold all my data. This hard drive held 5.4 megabytes. Imagine, more than an entire Bible on just one disk! It was hard to comprehend.

Software continued to change, and it wasn't long before my computer began to lose its glamor. I ran out of space, and new computers made mine seem as ancient as a dinosaur. I still remember the first time I saw a computer monitor showing a picture. It looked like science fiction and stirred new thoughts. I had never made a connection between a computer and a television, but suddenly people were talking about the possibilities. Could computers be used for more than just business?

In the early 1990s I upgraded again. By now these little hard drives could hold almost a gigabyte of data, or 1,000 megabytes. This was equivalent to over 200 Bibles on one disk, or 5,000 times more than my first floppy disks held! The salesman confidently stated that computer developers were reaching the end of their ability to cram more information on a disk. "There just isn't enough physical space on a hard drive to go past one gigabyte," he assured me.  Once again I returned home, confident we were reaching the end of this rapid growth in electronic storage capability. Of course, as we are all aware today, the industry was just getting started. Today you can purchase key chain flash drives capable of holding thousands of Bibles. And if the past is any indicator, we are nowhere near the end of this progression.

During this same period, other significant breakthroughs were happening in computing, not least of which was processing speed. Gordon Moore was a co-founder of Intel, an early pioneer of integrated circuit boards, commonly known as computer chips. In 1965 he predicted that the industry would double the number of transistors on one square inch of chip every year. In 1975 he adjusted this prediction to doubling every two years. He anticipated that the industry would make computers increasingly cheaper, faster, and useful for purposes men hadn't even dreamed of yet. This audacious forecast was scoffed at by many, but for the past forty years it has held true.

To get a better picture of this exponential change, imagine the same progression in the field of transportation. If automotive technology had advanced at the same rate, cars today would travel at 300,000 miles per hour, get over two million miles per gallon, and cost only four cents each![1] While the ability to store data was growing, the ability to process this information was increasing at an even more astounding rate. Computers have become cheaper, faster, and smaller simultaneously. This has greatly impacted our lives, our occupations, and even how we learn and access information.

When I was young boy, we had a set of *Britannica Senior Encyclopedias*, and if I had a question on any topic, I knew where to go. I remember looking up in amazement at that row of books on the top shelf in my father's office. I loved to stand on tiptoe on a chair, get a volume down, and explore. Each volume held an unbelievable mass of knowledge. But paper encyclopedias are largely a thing of the past, and the last printed *Britannica* was issued in 2010. Why would people spend money for clunky books when they have access to all this and more at their fingertips for free? After all, the *Britannica* only had 32,640 pages[2] and was outdated before the printing was completed; who wants that when billions of continually updated webpages are available online?

Constant Change

Life consists of change. I face each day understanding that it will not be an exact replica of the one before. Circumstances, challenges, and decisions will be different, and I accept this. If today were a repeat of yesterday, something would be dreadfully wrong. But there is one caveat; I don't like too much change too fast. Yet for many of us, that describes the world we live in. Can you imagine someone from the 1800's picking up one of today's newspapers? In just a short time, our world has experienced a massive upheaval beyond anything previous generations imagined. Standards of morality, belief in God, and even the public's view of truth—everything is up for grabs. Mores of society that seemed immovable, like the definitions of marriage or gender identity, are suddenly open for debate. All of this has created a confusing world in which to live and raise a family, and the constant change of electronic technology only generates more challenges.

Electronic Explosion

Every week seems to bring another gadget, a new device, or some product we've never heard of and didn't know we needed. Those of us who lived during the end of the twentieth century witnessed an electronic explosion unlike the world has ever seen. Communication, transportation, entertainment, and traditional marketplaces were affected. Our language has been altered, with social media and texting spawning a lingo of their own. Young people communicate using a dialect of words and phrases that were non-existent just a few years ago. I grew up never hearing words like megabyte or gigabyte. Checking for mail meant walking down the lane to a little black box with a red flag. All that has changed, and Google, something I once knew nothing about, is now a common verb in the English language.

Those of us desiring to follow Jesus and chart a safe course for ourselves and our children are constantly faced with tremendous challenges. Changes are coming fast, so how do we know which path to take? Every decision will have consequences, but how can we know what they are? It is tempting to assume we are the first generation to deal with this, but as we look at the effect of technology on humanity and the church, we will see our generation isn't the first to raise an alarm about its negative impact.

CHAPTER TWO

WHERE WILL THIS LEAD?

Throughout history, men have expressed alarm about change. The writer of Ecclesiastes warns against assuming "that the former days were better than these."[a] Yet we look back on those days and wonder what changes they were so worried about. Progress moved so slowly back then; why the concern? Means of transportation, methods of communication, and tools required to pursue our occupations changed minimally for centuries. But leading up to the Industrial Revolution, as changes became more frequent, so did the cries of alarm.

Conrad Gessner, a well-respected Swiss scientist, became alarmed as he saw the rapid increase in technology and information among the public. After all, how much knowledge can any one man use, and what effect will this overload of information have on society? In other words, what will this lead to? In a revolutionary book[b] Gessner laid out his concerns, stating that this overabundance of information was both "confusing and harmful" to the mind. He called for total

---

[a] Ecclesiastes 7:10
[b] Gessner's book, *The Bibliotheca Universalis*, was the first attempt to list all the books that had been printed in the first century of printing.

government regulation, believing this was the only way to solve this pressing issue. It wasn't information that concerned him; it was information overload.

But Conrad Gessner never accessed Wikipedia or used electronic media. He died in 1565, and his concern was the "confusing and harmful abundance of books" coming off the Gutenberg press. It was just too much information for man to properly assimilate. So Gessner produced a book calling for government regulation to solve this dangerous situation, ironically adding to the proliferation of information that concerned him.[1] The following century, in 1680, German philosopher and mathematician Gottfried Leibniz expressed similar concerns about the number of books being printed.[2]

> How much knowledge can any one man use, and what effect will this overload of information have on society?

Newspapers

Alarm bells sounded again in the eighteenth century as newspapers became more common. Malesherbes, a French lawyer, pled with his government in 1775 to reconsider this dangerous innovation. He reminded them that the pulpit had historically been the primary source for information. Imagine what would happen to society if men were able to access the news in the privacy of their own homes? He projected that newspapers would destroy the strength of the public assembly, and consequently was greatly concerned for the future of his country.[3]

Public Schools

This fear of information overload wasn't confined to the proliferation of printed matter. In 1883, *The Sanitarian,* a New York weekly medical journal, warned against another hazardous innovation—the introduction of public schools. Placing children in confined classrooms and flooding them with information seemed risky. Excessive study was considered a leading cause of insanity at the time, and *The Sanitarian* argued that these schools "exhaust the children's brains and nervous systems with complex and multiple studies, and ruin their bodies by protracted imprisonment."[4] The consistent cry from the critics could be summarized like this: "Too much information is hazardous, and humans are incapable of handling it."

Transportation

Then new methods of transportation emerged, along with their critics. For thousands of years the fastest method of transportation was the horse. When the British Stockton-Darling railroad opened in 1825, it was met with great apprehension. This was the first public railway to use steam locomotives, and the thought of traveling at an incredible thirty miles per hour seemed horrifying. Speculations arose that moving that fast might "kill you in gruesome ways, such as your body melting."[5]

Each new method attempting to move men farther or faster—the locomotive, the automobile—encountered fresh scorn. Why not just leave things alone? But the attempts to soar like the birds brought more than scorn; they met with a deluge of fearful statements. Some newspapers were chastised openly for publishing accounts that encouraged readers to believe man might eventually fly. George Melville, U.S. Navy Rear Admiral, firmly stated what most people saw as obvious. "There is no basis for the ardent hopes and positive statements made as to the safety and successful use of the dirigible balloon or flying machine."[6]

Communications

Innovations in communications had their detractors as well. In December 1877 the editor of *The New York Times* decried this new technological contraption called the telephone. He saw it as a danger to humanity. In an editorial, he ferociously attacked this unfamiliar device that could transfer voices over a wire. In a recent experiment in Rhode Island, scientists had stretched wires across four miles, and people on one end had listened to all manner of sounds coming from the other. According to rumor, this included "things which they did not venture to openly repeat!" As final proof that his fears were not exaggerated, the editor quoted a London writer who was also troubled by how the telephone would impact humanity. Gossip was bad enough, but what might happen if people could spread slander or intimate secrets without even being present? "We shall soon be nothing but transparent heaps of jelly to each other,"[7] he lamented. He didn't mind some change, but the telephone was taking things too far, too fast!

All through history, each time a revolutionary technological change has been invented, critics have tried to stop the progress. Fearful of where this might lead, they felt it their duty to sound an alarm.[c] Perhaps no group has been so noted for abhorrence of change as a band of English peasants who lived in the early 1800s.

The Luddites

At the beginning of the nineteenth century, British working families were struggling to survive. England's ongoing war with Napoleon's France had plunged the country's economy into recession, and poverty was rampant. Food ran short, jobs were few, and the working class was frustrated. Adding to their vexation was the fact that local textile manufacturers were replacing manual jobs with machinery. Work was already scarce; what would happen if the few available jobs disappeared because of mechanical innovations? As the working populace discussed this problem, anger rose.

One of the primary catalysts was the stocking frame, a knitting machine that produced fabric faster than hand-knitted material.

---

[c] One of these warnings is an amazingly prophetic science fiction book titled *The Machine Stops*. Authored by E.M. Forster in 1908, the short book tells of a world where everyone is basically online twenty-four hours a day, able to communicate with anyone around the globe, and everyone lives underground in his or her own little cubicle. People can travel by airship around the globe if they desire, but they have lost interest. Every place is the same inside the machine, and physical face-to-face relationships are a thing of the past. One young man wants to break out of this technological world . . . It is disturbing that someone over one hundred years ago foresaw the dangers of what electronic technology might do to humanity.

According to British laborers, machine-made fabric was low quality. If consumers became accustomed to this cheap, inferior fabric, the laborers feared their jobs would be lost. Public rallies were held, passionate speeches were delivered, and finally on March 11, 1811, the government moved against these activists. Soldiers broke up a crowd of protestors near Nottingham, and in response the angry workers tore through a local factory, smashing machinery. This turned into a full-scale riot covering a seventy-mile-wide swath of Northern England. Many rioters and soldiers were killed, and factories were vandalized, with some burnt to the ground. The primary focus of the destruction was this newfangled equipment. The workers saw the modern machinery as the primary cause of their economic depression, and by smashing stocking frames, they must have felt they were addressing the root cause of their ills.

These rioters had a hero named Ned Ludd. As the story goes, Ludd was a knitter in the city of Leicester. One day in a fit of anger toward these mechanical innovations, he grabbed a hammer and flattened a stocking frame. Throughout England, Ned Ludd became a symbolic champion for the frustrated workers. Historians today insist that Ned Ludd never existed,[8] but this didn't stop the stories.

Even today the Luddite legend lives on. People objecting to technological innovations are labeled as Luddites. These are the people who rise up and say, "Progress has gone far enough. Why can't we leave well enough alone?" But were the Luddites effective? Did they slow the advance of the Industrial Age or help their economic situation? No, they didn't achieve either goal. Fighting change isn't that simple; attempts to squelch technological change are rarely effective. The Luddites' fears may have been valid, but their methods were ineffective. Today, as in the past, people are raising their voices in alarm, many of them from a purely secular perspective.

Electronic Luddites

In 2005 CNN published an article proclaiming, "E-mails hurt IQ

Linked Technology

During the 1700's inventors began to see the potential in using steam power, followed by rapid advances in internal combustion engines in the 1800s. In the late 1800s men like William Armstrong began exploring hydraulics. Eventually the basic hoe was linked through hydraulics to the internal combustion engine, and the hoe became an excavator. Those who were developing engines or hydraulic systems couldn't have imagined the result but were unknowingly contributing to it. Then men developed satellites, rockets to launch them, and global positioning systems (GPS). Link all of this together and you have an excavator that knows where to dig precise trenches on a building site. But it all started with a basic hoe. There was no conceivable way those who worked on developing each innovation could have understood the power of the product that would be created with linked technology.

Linked technology, sometimes referred to as technological convergence, is evident in newer inventions like mobile phones. When they first came out, owning one seemed out of reach for anyone who wasn't wealthy, and using them for anything beyond conversation was inconceivable. But all that has changed. Phones became computers and were linked to data storage, then combined with cameras and GPS systems. They were made easy to use with touch screen technology, and finally connected to the Internet. Through linking, unimaginable possibilities became reality, and these little gadgets became useful, affordable tools for all levels of society.

Recently I was in India, and in Kolkata there is an area where day laborers looking for employment gather in huge crowds each morning. I asked some of them about their lives, what kind of work they were hoping for, and how much they could expect to earn that day, assuming an employer came along. The going rate for a construction worker in Kolkata was the American equivalent of $3 per day, and all of them were prepared to work hard all day to earn this miniscule wage. I was clearly among poverty-stricken people, so I was shocked when one Hindu woman pulled out her smartphone and asked if she could take my picture! Here was a woman who was struggling to feed her family, willing to work for $3 per day, yet carrying technology that just a few years ago was barely affordable.

Where Is All This Going?

Are we finally at a place where inventions will taper off and new discoveries diminish? Have we reached a plateau, like the computer salesman assured me in the early 1990s, where electronic technology has gone about as far as it can go? I don't think any of us believe that, but I don't think we understand how rapidly things will continue to change.

There was a time when computers just did what men told them to do. They were held back by our ability to conceive and improve, but this is changing rapidly. Now computers can learn from past mistakes, create new software, communicate between themselves, and even write their own code. One tech writer said, "Our machines are starting to speak a different language now, one that even the best coders can't fully understand."[2] This is frightening to some, and it presents a question: Is the day coming when we will serve the technologies originally created to serve us?

> Is the day coming when we will serve the technologies originally created to serve us?

Robotic Advances

Consider advances in robotic technology. Robots are accomplishing many things that seemed impossible until recently. But one human capability that robots have never achieved is reproduction. However, multiple teams are working to develop robots capable of both repairing and reproducing themselves. Do we understand the implications? When robots become faster, smarter, and capable of dominating humans, what kind of a world will that be? Not long ago this was science fiction material, but now some scientists who work in these fields are expressing alarm.

Robert Freitas works at the Institute for Molecular Manufacturing in Palo Alto and is the co-author of a book on self-replicating machines. As he has seen the rapid changes taking place in the robotic world, he has spoken out with concern. According to him, "As a matter of public policy, artificial machine systems should not be built that evolve, so that there can be no danger of them escaping our control."[3] This is a future no longer confined to science fiction novels.

Merging Man and Machine

Elon Musk has been involved in cutting edge technology for years. PayPal, SpaceX, and the Tesla electric car company are a few of the enterprises he has been instrumental in creating. In 2016 Musk co-founded a new company called Neuralink whose goal is to integrate the human brain with the computer.

Your brain is thinking much faster than your fingers can type or your mouth can speak. So why not bypass this slow interface and connect your brain directly to your computer? Imagine how much faster you could work and communicate. Musk sees this as a great blessing to people with disabilities from strokes or severe brain injuries. But Musk is also looking down the road to the time the human brain will no longer be able to compete with computers developed by artificial intelligence. "Artificial intelligence and machine learning will create computers so sophisticated and godlike that humans will need to implant 'neural laces' in their brains to keep up,"[4] Musk stated at a recent conference.

The Value of Information

One of the most amazing recent changes is how this focus on electronics has impacted the financial markets and what we view as valuable. Consider the significance people place on electronic technology and its ability to store, transfer, and process information.

Until recent years, wealth was directly connected to production or ownership of physical assets. Wealthy individuals either owned large holdings of natural resources or factories capable of mass-producing goods. In the nineteenth century, Andrew Carnegie owned steel factories and controlled much of the world's steel production. Henry Ford masterminded assembly lines and made his wealth by producing inexpensive cars. Cornelius Vanderbilt made his fortune in transportation, moving products for a growing America by ship and rail, while John D. Rockefeller grew rich through the oil industry.

These men made their money by producing or providing some tangible product or service. Technology has changed all this, however. Today the world's wealthiest men are primarily involved in disseminating information. Some of their companies have huge stock value yet few tangible assets. A journalist, noting how technology has turned the economic world upside down, made this observation in 2015. "Uber, the world's largest taxi company, owns no vehicles. Facebook, the world's most popular media owner, creates no content. Alibaba, the most valuable retailer, has no inventory. And Airbnb, the world's largest accommodation provider, owns no real estate. Something interesting is happening."[5] Interesting indeed! Today *information* is king, and those who control it are seeing incredible growth. This is one more way that electronics are changing our world.

> Today information is king, and those who control it are seeing incredible growth.

Coming Change: Blessing or Curse?

For many years technology changed very little. Men worked with simple tools all their lives, and then their children continued using the same tools to provide for themselves. But today a book on technology is outdated before going to print. Is the net effect a blessing or a curse? How are we to gauge this?

Some inventions are universally accepted. I don't see anyone, even those who think technology is dangerous, refusing to use a hoe and insisting it is better to garden with their fingers. Printing is a relatively new invention, yet I haven't met anyone who has concluded that we shouldn't use books. We need to be realistic as we consider the future, because changes are going to come faster as each invention enables others.

CHAPTER FOUR

CATEGORIZING TECHNOLOGY

Earlier we defined technology as anything we do to make our lives easier or better. Before deciding whether technology is a blessing or curse, let's establish some categories so we can discuss it more effectively. There is overlap, but for the purposes of this book, we'll look at four basic types of technology.

1. **Physical strength and stamina extenders.** This group includes inventions like farming tools, the basic hammer, or vehicles for transportation. All of these do something that a man can do alone, but they improve his ability. Think about one of our early ancestors out in the field trying to move a heavy rock. In exasperation he tries using a branch as a lever, and he invents a new technology.

2. **Nature controllers.** This category is a little more complicated. In the area where I live, we have irrigation systems. There isn't enough rain during the summer to grow crops, so huge dams have been constructed

in the mountains to gather water from the melting snowpack. Canals and pipelines snake through the valley, bringing water to the farms and crops. This is an attempt to improve on what nature already does. Hybrid and genetically modified seeds are an example of this, as well as the huge improvements that have been made in healthcare. Whether or not you agree with these efforts, they are attempts to control natural processes with the goal of improving life.

3. **Sensory stretchers.** These are tools we use to extend our natural human senses. Binoculars, microscopes, video cameras, and telephones fall into this category. We have eyes, but we want to see farther, smaller, or around the corner; these tools allow us this capability. We want to hear more clearly and talk to people who live in other places, so we employ hearing aids, public address systems, and telephones. We can see, but not in the dark, so we've developed everything from headlights to flashlights to night goggles to assist our visual capability. Using technology, humans can see in the dark almost as well as a cat.

4. **Intellectual expanders.** Our minds have tremendous ability, but we want more. We post lists on the refrigerator to jog our memories, create clocks to help us structure our lives, and develop electronic calculators to assist with math. We build computers to help us process information, do our bookkeeping, and perform other tasks that make our life easier. These are all functions our minds are capable of accomplishing, but intellectual expanders do it better, faster, and more accurately.

The fourth category is what we usually think of when we mention technology. These intellectual expanders involved tools like ballpoint pens, inexpensive paper, slide rules to help engineers, and the abacus for early mathematicians. Today electronic technology has replaced all this and more. Not only are computers being used as intellectual expanders, they are also expanding the power of tools within the other three categories. All of this brings more questions. Is this rapid move toward electronics a good thing? Do we really want batteries in every tool we use? Are we solving problems or just creating new ones?

Unintended Consequences

Every invention comes with unforeseen ramifications—results that the original inventor couldn't have envisioned. The microbiologist who spends hours peering at bacteria under a microscope sees pond water differently than the housewife in Bangladesh who goes to the local pond for drinking water. The inventor of the microscope never considered this. Knowing that I can talk to relatives after they have left for their home in another state makes saying goodbye after a visit easy—far different than if I were living in the 1700s and knew I would probably never speak to them again. People who developed cell phones probably weren't thinking about how their invention would change the way people relate to others. Unknown to the inventors of today's products, they are doing more than just addressing the problem in focus. They are changing people's view of themselves, their fellow men, and the world, and they are also creating new problems.

Alberto Santos-Dumont was a wealthy Frenchman, and an early pioneer in the development of aircraft. He invented new types of balloons, developed powered dirigibles, and was intrigued with flight for many years. Alberto had a purpose behind his endeavors. He believed that air travel had great potential in promoting world peace. He refused to patent his inventions and freely shared his designs. He imagined a world where people could freely travel, and thus grasp how much they have in common with those living in different countries and cultures.

Alberto made great contributions to aviation technology. But after witnessing how some of his aircraft designs were used in World War 1 and the São Paulo Revolution of 1932, he spiraled into depression. He was unable to cope with the fact that the very invention he had envisioned bringing peace was instead being used to destroy life. Alberto ultimately committed suicide on July 23, 1932.[1] He was unprepared for the unintended consequences of this new technology. When a man goes about inventing a solution to a problem, he usually isn't thinking about the unforeseen outcomes, but they always exist.

Nearly 1.3 million people die each year in automobile crashes.[2] That is 3,287 deaths per day due to the invention of the automobile. Humanity is dealing with massive environmental threats and potential nuclear terrorism. Banks can have their clients' information compromised by a computer hacker living in a different country. None of this would be possible were it not for new inventions and advances in technology.

Every new technological "improvement" brings corresponding setbacks. This has caused Richard Rhodes, a cynical techno-critic, to ask, "How much of what we readily identify as progress in the urban-industrial society is really the undoing of evils inherited from the last round of technological innovation?"[3] An army of computer technicians are working diligently, simply trying to stay ahead of malicious hackers. Products are constantly being developed and new services offered to protect against these threats. None of this would be needed if the computer had never been invented.

What If an Improvement . . . Isn't?
I suspect all of us have wondered at times if all this new technology is worth it. Is it possible that, while trying to make our lives easier and better, we are actually making them more difficult and complex? While mopping water off the floor after the dishwasher comes to a grinding halt, I can't help but ask this question. The repairman cheerfully informs me that the needed part costs almost as much as buying a new dishwasher, and the warranty has just expired. Of course, the repairman still needs to be paid, and this nagging question keeps hounding me: Was washing dishes by hand really that difficult?

Perhaps these inventions do make life easier, and clearly many wives believe a dishwasher is in this category. But is easier always better? Is it better for children to go off and do their own thing rather than sing together while they wash and dry the dishes? From a spiritual perspective, are all these inventions beneficial? Our answers may differ, but these are questions we should continue asking. Each piece of technology needs to be analyzed closely, because each brings unintended consequences.

Many Anabaptist communities are concerned that more is being lost than gained, and this has kept them from quickly accepting new technologies. Jameson Wetmore, a social science researcher from Arizona State University, has researched why the Amish accept some technologies but not others. He found that, while the outside world sees innovations as good until proven otherwise, the Amish first decide whether a new technology might erode the very values they are trying to preserve. When Wetmore asked one Amish man why they were concerned about adopting new things, he responded, "Well, look what they did to you. Do you know the names of your neighbors? As soon as you have a car, you never talk to your neighbor again. That's not the society we want to live in."[4] From this Amish man's perspective, more was lost than gained with the ownership of a car.

Technology isn't going away, and I am amused when I see movements and organizations using technology to fight it. Ironically, the Luddites were famous for this. As they went through English textile factories swinging their sledgehammers, smashing machinery, and destroying stocking frames, history says they sang a little ditty: "Enoch made them, Enoch shall break them."[5] The message behind the song was simple. Enoch Taylor, owner of a blacksmith company, was the manufacturer of the stocking frames. But Enoch had also manufactured the sledgehammers they were wielding. They were using one type of technology to destroy another, but they had been using sledgehammers so long that they didn't seem like dangerous new innovations. We see similar situations today—websites decrying the advance of technology, or men promoting "back to nature" ideology, yet arriving in a car. If they really wanted to dispose of technology, why didn't they walk to the event?

So when is a technology dangerous, and when should we be alarmed?

Wendell Berry, an American novelist, cultural critic, and environmental activist, has dedicated his life to the suppression of technology. He speaks and writes with passion about how nice it was growing up on a farm in the 1940s, and you sense that, in his eyes, all the technology since then goes too far. About progress in farming he says, "The coming of the tractor made it possible for a farmer to do more work, but not better."[6] For Berry, this seems to be the criteria. When quantity is emphasized over quality, that is too far.

But who decides when the work is done better? Recently I talked to an Amish businessman who had just obtained permission from his bishop to purchase a CNC router for his business; the CNC router simply did a much better job. Others in his community disagree. They say this machine puts others out of work, and that isn't better. This is where the issue gets thorny. We don't all agree on which technology is a blessing and which a curse. Most of us like technology that has been around a long time, but are suspicious about recent inventions. A hoe invented many generations ago is just a tool. Nothing scary about that. But we tend to view recent inventions with suspicion, especially if they've arrived quickly. Some see new technology as unnecessary and a little frightening.[a]

Others of us like the new. We are excited when improved products roll out the door. We like the advantages and opportunities that come with these advances. But regardless of your personality, preference, or even concerns, one thing is certain—short of a major catastrophe or the return of the Lord, we are just seeing the beginning of technological advance. Electronics are speeding up the rate of change, and if the past is any indicator of the future, we need to be prepared. A digital tech tsunami is headed our way!

---

[a] This observation has caused computer scientist Alan Kay to wryly suggest; "Technology is anything that wasn't around when you were born." —Interview with Alan Kay, David Greelish, April 2, 2013, <http://techland.time.com/2013/04/02/an-interview-with-computing-pioneer-alan-kay/>, accessed on May 22, 2017.

CHAPTER FIVE

TECHNOLOGICAL CHANGE: DIFFERENT PERSPECTIVES

Most of us have picked a white dandelion puffball, marveled at its beauty and elegance, and blown its tiny seeds. Children search for these puffballs with excitement. Recently I overheard a child boasting that his lawn had more dandelions than his friend's lawn. We are capable of turning anything into a status symbol—even dandelions. Adults see the broad dandelion leaves shading out desirable grass, and are glad to see them go. But that view is a matter of opinion. The proud child and the frustrated gardener look at the same flower, but from completely different perspectives.

The same is true with technological advances. Some see them as threats to their family and way of life. Others see them as offering solutions to existing problems, and they can't wait to see what new discovery may be just around the corner. Even though inventions do bring some problems, these people are sure that new discoveries will soon address these issues as well.

There have always been people pushing for change and improvement, and others insisting "that the former days were better than these,"[a] but the arguments have intensified as the speed of innovation has increased.

These differences in perspective are more than just optimistic personalities seeing things differently from down-in-the-mouth pessimists. Neither is it just a difference in religious viewpoints. For many years both historians and philosophers have debated the role of technology in shaping cultures and civilizations. On one end of the spectrum is a group of people labeled determinists.

The Determinist

No one could accuse Ted Kaczynski of acting out of ignorance or being uneducated. With an undergraduate degree from Harvard, a PhD in mathematics from the University of Michigan, and a teaching job at the University of California, Berkeley, Ted Kaczynski had impressive academic credentials. But in the early 1970s, Kaczynski withdrew from society to a remote cabin in Montana, convinced that the world was on a downward spiral and would soon collapse. The cause? The advance of technology!

Ted Kaczynski stated that the "Industrial Revolution and its consequences have been a disaster for the human race."[1] He believed immediate action was necessary to keep technology from taking over modern civilization, so he resorted to violence. In 1978 Ted sent a mail bomb to a professor at Northwestern University in Illinois. Over the next seventeen years, he sent a total of sixteen bombs to unsuspecting individuals he believed were instrumental in advancing technology. By the time he was captured in 1996, Ted Kaczynski had injured twenty-three and killed three through his mail-bombing campaign.

While few individuals holding Ted's beliefs turn to violence as he did, many see technology as a dangerous force. Ted Kaczynski is a determinist, a person who believes that inventions initially appear as extensions of ourselves, tools created to serve us. But as time goes on, we begin to serve them. In other words, technology is at first

---

[a] Ecclesiastes 7:10

the servant, but eventually it becomes king.

Technological determinism can be compared to a seed. Picture a tomato seed. Even though it has no brain it always becomes a tomato plant when properly encouraged. In a sense, you could say a tomato seed "wants" to become a tomato plant. A determinist sees technology, electronic or otherwise, similarly. They see a force in technology that "wants" to dominate. This ultimately causes inventions to go beyond the inventor's initial intentions.

The Instrumentalist

On the other end of the spectrum is the instrumentalist. He sees technology as neutral and completely subservient to the desires of the user. Many of us like this view. One author has said, "Instrumentalism is the most widely held view of technology, not least because it's the view we would prefer to be true. The idea that we're somehow controlled by our tools is anathema to most people."[2]

Those endorsing technological change have heavily promoted the instrumentalist view. One of these was David Sarnoff, an early pioneer of American radio and television and president of Radio Corporation of America (RCA). Sarnoff advised a conservative and skeptical public that there was nothing to fear from these innovations. During a speech at Notre Dame, he explained the situation like this: "We are too prone to make technological instruments the scapegoats for the sins of those who wield them. The products of modern science are not in themselves good or bad; it is the way they are used that determines their value."[3] David Sarnoff was an instrumentalist, believing innovations are just tools with no inherent power of their own.

When you are familiar with a piece of technology, it is hard to see anything other than a tool created to make life easier or better. The radio and television were just tools designed to transfer information. But when you step back and look at the effects of what then seemed like benign inventions, you have to wonder if something else is going on.

The Inevitablist

There is yet another viewpoint promoted today—that technological advance is naturally occurring proof of evolution. Those who endorse Charles Darwin's theory of survival of the fittest see a stepped-up version of this in the advance of technology. Inevitability sees our world gradually getting better. Inventions are introduced into the marketplace, and like Darwin's theory, only the fittest survive. Our garages, storage sheds, and landfills hold the many intermediary inventions that were surpassed by something "better."

Author Kevin Kelly vocally promotes inevitability. He encourages us to get out of the way and let this force have free rein. "If the things we make will get better the next time, that means that the golden age is ahead of us, and not in the past."[4] Kelly believes we "have a moral obligation to increase the best of technology. When we enlarge the variety and reach of technology, we increase options not just for ourselves and not just for others living but for all those to come as the technium ratchets up complexity and beauty over generations."[5] For the inevitablist, the force that drives change is a wonderful thing. Technology is evolving through natural selection, and its benefits are further proof, for some, that there is no God.

Technology: How Should We View It?

So how are followers of Jesus to view technology? Is it simply an extension of man, and evil only because of who wields it? Or is there a force within these inventions that we don't understand and can't explain? Further, is it possible that things have changed? Could it be that as technology advances, it controls us in ways we don't understand?

Even before the rapid proliferation of electronic gadgetry we are dealing with today, men wrestled with this question. Dietrich Bonhoeffer, in an unfinished book titled *Ethics,* which was edited and published after his death in 1949, tried to encapsulate this concern.

> From the Egyptian pyramids to the Greek temples, from the medieval cathedrals up to the eighteenth

century, technology was a matter of handicraft. It served religion, royalty, culture, and people's daily needs. The technology of the modern West has freed itself from every kind of service. Its essence is not the service but mastery over nature. A wholly new spirit has produced it, the spirit of violent subjection of nature to thinking and experimenting human beings; . . . Technology has become an end in itself.[6]

To Bonhoeffer, something fundamental had changed. He was seeing a shift from the neutral instrumentalism of the past to the dominating determinism of technology in his day. What might he say if he were still alive?

Impact on Mental and Physical Health

We might not all agree on what force is driving change, but it is certain that technology is changing our lives more than we could have predicted fifty years ago. It is also affecting our health. A Nielson Company report in 2016 found that American adults were spending over ten and a half hours in front of a screen each day.[7] This includes time spent on smartphones, personal computers, video games, tablets, televisions, and other multimedia devices. One must stop and wonder what this is doing to our minds, our health, and views of reality. Another study revealed that the average adult in America is physically active only seventeen minutes each day.[8]

Consider the changes in medicine. In 2015 researchers found that nearly three in five American adults take a prescription drug, and the percentage of people taking five or more had nearly doubled since 2012.[9] The report went on to say that one of the leading factors in this uptick is obesity. Americans are gaining weight, partly due to their use of electronic technology, and then turning to medical advances to fix the problem. One can't help but wonder how much of this would change if people would simply turn off their devices and take a walk.

In April 2017 *National Geographic* produced a lengthy article on some of the technological advances that are shaking and shaping our modern society. As the thought-provoking piece concludes, the writer describes how technology is increasingly intertwined in our lives:

> Virtual reality headsets are one of the hottest selling gamer toys. Our cars are our feet, our calculators are our minds, and Google is our memory. Our lives now are only partly biological, with no clear split between the organic and the technological, the carbon and the silicon. We may not know yet where we're going, but we've already left where we've been.[10]

These studies are being performed by secular researchers and only focus on how technology is affecting our physical lives. If even the secular world is concerned about these changes, how are followers of Jesus to view them? Is suspicion of new things simply surrender to unrealistic fear? Is it a lack of faith? Sometimes I feel inner discomfort when I see a new electronic gadget. Am I just being a Luddite, a worrier who doesn't like change and believes "that the former days were better than these?"[b] Or is it possible that some of this apprehension is a healthy, realistic concern? Could it be that some of these technological advances are threatening our spiritual lives in ways we struggle to articulate?

> Our cars are our feet, our calculators are our minds, and Google is our memory.

---

[b] Ecclesiastes 7:10

CHAPTER SIX

ARE ALL TOOLS CREATED EQUAL?

On our kitchen counter sits a large wooden knife holder. My wife keeps it high off the floor and away from the front of the counter for a very good reason. Knives are dangerous technology. Maybe you have never considered a butcher knife to be technology. But remember, technology is "science or knowledge put into practical use to solve problems or invent useful tools." And if you have ever tried to butcher a cow or cut meat without a knife, you will quickly discover that this technology is very useful. In fact, the Bible speaks of a group of people who longed for this type of "cutting edge" technology.

Saul was king, and Israel longed for the day when they could overthrow the Philistines who oppressed them and made their lives miserable. How were the Philistines keeping Israel under their thumb? By restricting their access to technology. Notice how the Bible describes their plight.

> Now there was no smith found throughout all the land of Israel: for the Philistines said, Lest the Hebrews

make them swords or spears: [20]But all the Israelites went down to the Philistines, to sharpen every man his share, and his coulter, and his axe, and his mattock. [21]Yet they had a file for the mattocks, and for the coulters, and for the forks, and for the axes, and to sharpen the goads. [22]So it came to pass in the day of battle, that there was neither sword nor spear found in the hand of any of the people that were with Saul and Jonathan: but with Saul and with Jonathan his son was there found.[a]

Can you imagine the constant frustration and humiliation? The Israelites had a history of conquering. They had made their own tools, created weapons, and won many battles in the past. But those days were gone. Now, every time a Jewish man needed a tool repaired, he was reminded of Philistine oppression. He had to take that tool to a heathen blacksmith. And due to the Israelites limited access to technology, there seemed little hope of overcoming the Philistines. You may not think of a sharp knife as the latest in technology, but they did!

Risky Technology

We grow up understanding that butcher knives are useful but also dangerous. We don't leave them lying around on the floor or give them to small children to play with. We put them in drawers, store them safely in sheaths, or place them up high where those who lack maturity will not be able to access them. Technology comes with risk, and generally, the more powerful the technology, the more its propensity for harm. Yet we don't stop using it. I have never found a person who has concluded that butcher knives are too dangerous to use, or who has decided to use his hands to tear meat apart to avoid the hazard. No, all of us use knives. We have concluded that their usefulness outweighs the hazard. But we are extremely careful *how* they are used.

So how does this logic play out in our use of electronic tools?

---

[a] 1 Samuel 13:19–22

Electronic Tools

In 2016 *Time* magazine published an article titled "The 50 Most Influential Gadgets of All Time." Their tech department categorized recent inventions, not by their complexity or the creativity of the inventor, but according to how each has impacted society. The article works up through fifty inventions, culminating with the device they concluded has been most influential on our culture: Apple's smartphone, the iPhone.

The first iPhone was unveiled to the public on January 9, 2007, after several years of intense, secretive development. When Steve Jobs stepped onto the stage in San Francisco to demonstrate the iPhone, no one could have predicted how much impact it would have on society. Many Apple engineers sitting in the audience just hoped that this barely tested prototype didn't crash on its debut. But it succeeded, and this powerful device, famous for its intuitive way of interacting with the user, became Apple's best-known product and a tremendous financial success for the company. *Time* magazine concluded their appraisal of the device by saying, "The iPhone popularized the mobile app, forever changing how we communicate, play games, shop, work, and complete many everyday tasks. . . . But, more than that, it fundamentally changed our relationship to computing and information—a change likely to have repercussions for decades to come."[1]

Without question, the iPhone is a powerful tool. The device is an excellent example of "technological convergence."[b] In addition to the phone's original goal of placing calls, the user can send emails, read books, use social media, surf the Internet, listen to the radio,

---

[b] Technological convergence is the movement toward combining different technologies in a single device. As technologies are added, the power of the device can be increased exponentially.

send text messages, take pictures, watch movies, pay bills, watch television, find your location with its GPS, and more.

Inherent Danger

As all of us are aware, a smartphone is not just a useful tool. Like a butcher knife, it comes with inherent dangers. Mobile phones are relatively inexpensive and simple to use, and the average amount of time people are spending on their phones continues to rise. In 2015 the average user was spending 1.85 hours (111 minutes) per day on his mobile device. That is an increase of 40 minutes per day since 2012, just three years earlier.[2] With the Internet waiting to deliver a mass of ungodly material, and devices capable of providing it quickly and conveniently, the threat is clear. Many individuals admit they have used the smartphone to connect with sites that have been destructive to their marriages and spiritual lives. Many have found themselves ensnared by the curse of pornography. A young man once had to face a store clerk to purchase this illicit material, but now he can access explicit websites in the privacy of his car or bedroom.

Pornography on the Internet has become a huge problem. Researchers tell us that 40 million people in America regularly visit porn sites and 35 percent of all Internet downloads are related to pornography. That is an enormous exposure to ungodly material. Even more disturbing, search engines get 116,000 queries every day related to child pornography.[3] The same iPhone that can be an amazingly useful tool can become a deceptive snare.

Equal Danger?

Does a butcher knife pose the same level of risk as a constant electronic companion capable of delivering spiritually destructive content at all hours of the day and night? This will depend on our point of reference. For an unbeliever, perhaps there is little difference. Many may even have more fear of the sharp knife than the iPhone. But what about a follower of Jesus Christ battling Satan's temptations? He knows he is weak but has a strong desire to live a holy life. Is the risk between these two tools similar for him?

Of course not! While using a butcher knife carries the risk of physical injury, the iPhone comes with access to material that could be devastating to his spiritual life, his family relationships, and his eternal destiny. The danger with both is very real, but the hidden danger packed into that iPhone is much greater, a fact to which many could give personal testimony. But let's change the question. Let's suppose that the iPhone can no longer access harmful material.

Filtered Internet

The Internet is simply a global system of interconnected computer networks. It began with a goal of providing a method for educational institutions and military installations to communicate with each other, and during the 1980s this was its primary function. In the early 1990s commercial interests began to take notice, and by the late 1990s it became evident that this global network was going to be much larger than anyone had imagined. Just a few years after public access was granted, it became obvious that some sort of filter would be needed. On December 21, 2000, the Children's Internet Protection Act (CIPA) was signed, requiring all schools and libraries in the United States to install Internet filters as a condition for federal funding. Since that time, filters have become much more powerful and adept at sifting out undesirable content. They are not perfect, but there are some very good ones that can help users more safely navigate the Internet. With this in mind, let's compare an iPhone with a butcher knife again.

Are All Tools Equal?

Let's assume that your iPhone has a perfect Internet filter. It is now incapable of downloading explicit material or accessing questionable websites. Gone is the fear of accidently connecting with some site that might tempt or lead down a wrong path. We agreed earlier that both butcher knives and smartphones are useful tools with potential hazards. But have we now equalized the risk? Does a good filtering system mitigate your fears of electronic technology? And if not, why? Are you, like the Luddites back in England who were fearful of the new stocking frame, simply giving in to fear? Is your concern a lack of faith?

I have talked to many people who have strong fears about the Internet and electronic technology, and I believe some of their fears are unwarranted. It is possible to overanalyze new advances and see major problems behind every invention. History shows this clearly. Almost every time a new technique or technology has appeared, there have been those on the sideline with furrowed brows, shaking their heads and refusing to participate. Is this simply history repeating itself?

Possibly, but before we decide that those concerned about electronic technology are paranoid, I believe we must look closer and examine other ways we are being affected.

> It is possible to overanalyze new advances and see major problems behind every invention. History shows this clearly.

PART TWO

2

IS SOMETHING ELSE HAPPENING HERE?

CHAPTER SEVEN

VITAL RELATIONSHIPS: THE CORE OF WHO WE ARE

"Sally" is a friend from our local community. She has had many struggles, and several people in her past have let her down. Occasionally she visits our home, and we have spent hours trying to understand the pain caused by her dysfunctional relationships. Partially due to her past, Sally has empathy for pain in all creatures, and seeing an abandoned stray cat is more than she can bear. She knows what it feels like to be abandoned. Consequently, Sally has an abundance of cats in her house.

Recently Sally had a question. "Why is it that you church people don't have the same concern for cats that I do? You are supposed to be more loving than people like me, yet I am the one taking care of all these abandoned cats." This question has led to several lengthy discussions and some introspection. Why don't I value stray cats like Sally does? Further, why do we place different values on different forms of life? Why don't I regard cats in the same way I do humans? Even within the animal kingdom, I tend to value some animals more than others.

Some have argued that our life value system has to do with

complexity. A dog, for example, seems more complex and closer to humans than a beetle. Consequently, we feel little discomfort when smashing an insect, yet are uncomfortable seeing a puppy in pain. While this may provide some explanation, there are some major problems with this view. The "simple" housefly, for example, is an intricately designed creature, and the closer you look, the more complex it gets. With more than three thousand eyes capable of seeing in all directions, it's hardly fair to call it simple! Yet most of us can swat a housefly with little remorse or thought about the amazing complexity we have just destroyed. So how do we determine the value of various forms of life? How do we establish the worth of a human life versus a cat, a monkey, or the common housefly? And how do we determine the proper relationship we should have with each?

Our Reference for Relationship

If you are an evolutionist, then asking whether a housefly or a human has more value is an excellent question. After all, if life is a meaningless byproduct of a cosmic accident, then who is to decide which has more value? We are seeing the results of this value system in our society. But if you believe in the God of the Bible, this changes everything. That humans have more value than animals is clear throughout Scripture. From the beginning, man was to have dominion over animals. Interwoven through the Old Testament is the fact that animals were created to be under man's dominion and were for his good.[a] This was not intended as a license for abuse, but as guidance for determining the value we place on animals. Whether talking about people, material things, or religions, it is critical that we closely examine the value we place on each. When you start tampering with relationships, you are touching the core of who we are

---

[a] Genesis 1:26; Psalm 104:14

as humans, and as people move further away from a Biblical worldview, the results are not pretty.

On April 3, 2018, Nasim Najafi walked into YouTube's corporate office and began firing a gun at office staff, injuring three before killing herself. An investigation revealed that Nasim was angry with the company for not posting or paying for her videos, so she decided to act. Journalists who covered the story interviewed her family, trying to determine what kind of person would walk into an office and randomly start shooting strangers. Her father described her as "a vegan activist and animal lover. As a youngster, she would not even kill ants that invaded the family home, instead using paper to remove them to the back yard."[1] It's incredible that a woman who was opposed to killing ants was willing to kill people! Her values were obviously not attached to a Biblical worldview.

Two Vital Relationships

Much of Jesus' teaching centered on values and relationships. Whether His topic related to earthly wealth[b] or receiving honor from men,[c] Jesus clearly identified two relationships as most important. In this interaction between Jesus and a scribe, notice the relationships Jesus emphasizes.

> And one of the scribes came, and having heard them reasoning together, and perceiving that he had answered them well, asked him, Which is the first commandment of all? [29]And Jesus answered him, The first of all the commandments is, Hear, O Israel; The Lord our God is one Lord: [30]And thou shalt love the Lord thy God with all thy heart, and with all thy soul, and with all thy mind, and with all thy strength: this is the first commandment. [31]And the second is like, namely this, Thou shalt love thy neighbor as thyself. There is none

---
[b] Luke 12:13–21
[c] Matthew 6:1-4

other commandment greater than these. ³²And the scribe said unto him, Well, Master, thou hast said the truth: for there is one God; and there is none other but he: ³³And to love him with all the heart, and with all the understanding, and with all the soul, and with all the strength, and to love his neighbor as himself, is more than all whole burnt offerings and sacrifices. ³⁴And when Jesus saw that he answered discreetly, he said unto him, Thou art not far from the kingdom of God. And no man after that durst ask him any question."ᵈ

This is an astounding passage! If a man is going to flourish, his relationships with both God and others must be correct. Jesus even said that all the law and the prophets depend on this!ᵉ Think back over the Old Testament. Consider God's efforts in working with mankind through the centuries. Think of the animal sacrifices, the building of altars, the construction of the temple, and all the religious activities of man—a tremendous expenditure of energy and resources. Yet none of that is as important as how a man relates to God and his fellow men.

At times, I become weary of this word *relationship*. Our culture is very feelings-oriented, and a great amount of time is spent making sure everyone feels good and has healthy interaction. If we think we have been treated improperly, we rush off to our counselor, tell him how our feelings have been hurt, and discuss our relationships. The primary focus seems to be how *I* am feeling and how people are relating to *me*.

But Jesus' focus is on how I relate to God and my fellow man, rather than on how they relate to me. The important issue isn't how much I am valued, but rather, what my values are. Do I actually see God as preeminent? Is fulfilling His will my highest desire? Do I truly love

---

ᵈ Mark 12:28–34
ᵉ Matthew 22:40

my fellow man? If man can get these two relationships right, Jesus says everything else will fall into place. Conversely, when these are out of sync, everything else in our lives will spin out of control.

> The important issue isn't how much I am valued, but rather, what my values are.

How does this relate to our use of technology? Some threats from technology are easily recognizable. For example, it is not difficult to identify the danger in pornography. We know it has devastating repercussions in the lives of many men, on marriages, and on the very moral fabric of our society. But are there more subtle threats?

More Than Meets the Eye?

Let's look more closely at some less obvious ways electronic technology impacts us. First, how can these devices change our view of God and His kingdom? How can they distract us from the glory of His majesty? We need to scrutinize anything that could distort our vision of God.

We also want to look at how technology can affect the second relationship Jesus mentioned—how we view, value, and communicate with each other. How is this impacting the local church?

Finally, given the great capacity these devices have to shape how we think about God and each other, there are some questions each of us should be asking. How should a follower of Jesus relate to electronic technology? Is it blessing my walk with God? Jesus says that how we relate to God and man is extremely important. If we are going to survive the pressures of our day, we must closely guard these two relationships.

CHAPTER EIGHT

GOD AND GOOGLE

Every human on this earth longs for transcendent relationship and searches for something larger and more powerful. Men have always faced obstacles; we have an inherent desire for a god who is capable of stepping in to fix our issues. Humanity has worshiped the sun, the moon, mountains, and even animals, trees, and geographic locations. Men, in their search for a living god, have even worshiped other humans,[a] declaring that certain emperors or kings are immortal and can fill the inner void for transcendence. Today sports figures, movie actors, and rock stars are worshiped. But eventually all these men die, proving that they are mortal just like those who worship them.

The God of the Bible has revealed Himself to mankind in many ways. God desires that men worship only Him, but there are some struggles with this relationship. First, this living God almost always remains invisible. Mankind doesn't like that. He likes to see what he is worshiping! Second, this living God demands not only outward

---

[a] Acts 12:22

worship, but also obedience and personal accountability. Every human who longs to interact with the living God resists submitting to His will. So in man's quest for a god who fills his inner longing but doesn't require too much accountability, man has turned to other things.

One of the most perplexing traits of humanity is our tendency to worship objects made with our own hands. As foolish as it may sound, we see this throughout the Old Testament and in many parts of the world today. Men make images and idols from wood and stone, bow down to them, and proclaim their greatness. Over and over, the prophets called this foolish. They appealed to both God's law and human rationale. Notice the logic in Psalm 115. The writer describes the absurdity of worshiping something that isn't alive and has no power or ability!

> Their idols are silver and gold, the work of men's hands. [5]They have mouths, but they speak not: eyes have they, but they see not: [6]They have ears, but they hear not: noses have they, but they smell not: [7]They have hands, but they handle not: feet have they, but they walk not: neither speak they through their throat. [8]They that make them are like unto them; so is every one that trusteth in them.[b]

Why look to some dead object for help when it has less ability than you do? This inclination demonstrates our pressing need to worship something, even if it's only a carving. But the Psalmist doesn't end there. He continues: "O Israel, trust thou in the LORD: he is their help and their shield."[c]

Instead of bowing down and trusting in a god that can't speak, hear, smell, or move—a god less intelligent than you—worship the living Creator! Worship the God who created the universe and has

---

[b] Psalm 115:4–8
[c] Psalm 115:9

the power to do something about your problems! That should be the obvious conclusion. But of course, we are back to the original difficulty: This living God still calls for submission and accountability. We don't like to be called into question for our actions. What man really longs for is something powerful enough to address his needs, while allowing him to live as he pleases.

Many feel they have found this in technology, particularly the Internet. It is a powerful force and provides answers to man's questions; many see it as the best path to a better world. Notice author Kevin Kelly's observation. "In all cultures prior to the seventeenth century or so, the quiet, incremental drift of progress was attributed to the gods, or to the one God. It wasn't until progress was liberated from the divine and assigned to ourselves that it began to feed upon itself."[1]

In this author's view, the advance of technology increased when men freed themselves from the notion of a god outside of themselves. Now we have something made with our own hands that is finally making our world a better place. While looking to the Internet as the answer to the world's problems may be hard to initially grasp, notice the qualities of the Internet and consider why men might be tempted to trust and even worship this powerful force.

Omnipresent. There is a strong push today to make the Internet a global force available to everyone. Just a few years ago this seemed unattainable. People hadn't even been able to get telephone wires into many remote places. Now wireless communication has removed this obstacle, and the word "omnipresent," at one time only attributed to God, is being used for the Internet. One leader in wireless capability says, "If I can operate Google, I can find anything, anywhere, anytime. Which is why I say that Google, combined with Wi-Fi, is a little bit like God. God is wireless, God is everywhere, and God sees and knows everything."[2]

Never before in the history of man has anything other than God claimed this kind of omnipresence.

Eternally Secure. Because it is spread across many countries on countless servers, the Internet would be very difficult to stop. A power outage in one area might stop the flow of information from that region for a time, but the data wouldn't be lost. This gives users a sense of safety. Even the language used, such as putting your information "in the cloud" implies security beyond the problems humans deal with. While we live in fear of fire, floods, and other disasters that threaten our information, those who get their data "into the cloud" can rest. Everything will be okay forever, because the Internet can never turn off. According to Kelly, "If we wanted to turn off the Internet right now, it would not be easy to do . . . In many ways the Internet is designed to never turn off. Ever."[3]

All Knowing. You can ask Google any question. Regardless how difficult your inquiry is, there is one answer you will never receive. Google may respond with "No results found," but it will never tell you, "I don't know." It will always respond, thus people increasingly view the Internet as omniscient. You can ask "Who was Jesus Christ?" or "Who made God?" and it will immediately respond with an array of information. Then you can choose the answer that seems good to you. We like that! Finally, an all-knowing force willing to answer any difficult question but leave the final verdict up to us. And while our egocentric selves like this arrangement, even the secular world is alarmed at where this could lead. One psychologist from Harvard explains the problem like this:

> There's this crazy idea that all the billions of webpages have been thoroughly vetted and reviewed, and this omniscient source found the best. That whoever or whatever is doing the searching for us is infallible and omniscient. Google isn't necessarily giving you the best information, but what it thinks you want.[4]

Search engines like Google are designed to learn your preferences and deliver information based on past searches. While this can be helpful, it also slants the results we receive. For centuries man has been searching for a god like this! One that knows everything, responds quickly to any question, and provides answers that agree with our desires. Beautiful! Finally, a god that serves us! A powerful source that serves up information to fit our preconceived notions and desires! Contrast this to the Word of God, which pricks, pokes, and jabs at the conscience.

A Custom-Designed God

While traveling in Cambodia, I came across a large idol in the middle of the street. Vehicles were forced to detour around it. I couldn't help but marvel again at the foolishness of idol worship. Why would intelligent people line up, patiently waiting their turn to kneel before this chunk of brass? I felt like getting out of my vehicle and crying out, "Can't you see there is no life there? That thing can't speak, hear, move, think, or answer you! Why worship it?"

Then I had to stop and reflect. What if that idol could talk? What if it could answer any question? What if it could remember far better and respond faster than humans? Imagine a god that could do all this instantly. Can you understand why men could begin to view technology as something more than just a physical tool? Can you grasp why humans, created by God with a desperate need to worship, are turning to electronic technology to fill that need?

It's Not Affecting Me!

As I read articles and books concerning the advance of modern technology, I am sobered. It is obvious that many see continued advancement as the best hope for mankind. Many are trusting in technology just as men throughout history have bowed down to idols. Even as I researched, I consoled myself with thoughts like this: "While many are seeing electronic technology as a god, I am simply using it as a tool." In other words, "It might be dangerous for other folks, but I understand the danger. It's not affecting me." Am I really unaffected by technology? It is so easy to shake my head at others. But what if these electronic tools, which unquestionably make many tasks so much easier, are changing how I perceive God and my fellow man?

Impact on Our Relationship with God

As I have analyzed my own life, I have concluded that my use of technology has affected how I see God. It happens in subtle ways that I hardly realize. Technology provides effortless immediacy, whether operating a backhoe to move huge mountains of earth or asking Google a question and getting an instant reply. I like this, and before long, getting instant results seems normal. Then I struggle to understand why God doesn't respond as quickly as Google. This problem is a natural progression, because men struggled with God on this issue long before electronic technology showed up.

Waiting on God has always taxed man's patience. Scripture repeatedly exhorts men to wait on the Lord. Notice how David describes seeking after God. "Shew me thy ways, O LORD; teach me thy paths. Lead me in thy truth, and teach me: for thou art the God of my salvation; on thee do I wait all the day."[d]

Much of David's life was spent waiting. This wasn't easy, but in David's time it was normal. People spent a lot of time traveling on foot and preparing meals. News from a battlefield a few miles away took hours to reach them. Today, I live in an instant society. If the temperature in my house isn't just right, I adjust the thermostat and expect things to change instantly. If I want ice cubes, I go to the kitchen and assume I'll find them. If I need to contact someone, I pick up the phone and expect to talk to them instantly, regardless of where on the globe they live. David was not accustomed to instantaneous fulfillment of desires, yet he struggled with waiting on God. How much more impatient might he have been if he had lived in a culture of instant gratification? Living in an instant society affects what we expect from God and how we relate to Him.

---

[d] Psalm 25:4, 5

Avoiding Discipline

Wise men throughout the ages were known as men of discipline, and the Christian life is to be a disciplined walk. Throughout history, godly individuals were famous for rising early to meditate on Scripture, spending many hours in prayer, and seeking the face of God by fasting. They knew what it meant to patiently wait on answers from God. But where are the disciplined men today? And why should we bother with all this when answers to every conceivable question are readily available on Google?

> Living in an instant society affects what we expect from God and how we relate to Him.

In *The Tech-Wise Family*, Andy Crouch says it like this, "Because technology is primarily devoted to making our lives easier, it discourages us from disciplines, especially ones that involve disentangling us from technology itself."[5]

I propose that all of this is impacting our dependence on God and our relationship with Him more than we realize. If men of the past were willing to turn from God to worship idols carved from wood, how much care should we take to ensure that our hearts don't turn from the living God to technology? As Marshall McLuhan[e] said a long time ago, "We shape our tools and afterwards our tools shape us."[6]

Jesus said that our relationship with the Father is of utmost importance, and technology is threatening this vital relationship. Jesus also talked about a second relationship that is "like unto it."[f] In the next chapter we will look at how electronic technology is affecting this one.

---

[e] Marshall McLuhan was a Canadian professor and controversial author in the late 1960s. He wrote extensively on technology, the effects of media, and the impact of pop culture. He is also famous for predicting the World Wide Web, or the Global Village as he described it, decades before it arrived. An agnostic for years, McLuhan converted to Roman Catholicism after being influenced by the writings of G.K. Chesterton.

[f] Matthew 22:39

CHAPTER NINE

CONNECTED AND LONELY

People have an inner need for relationship with other people, but at the same time we want autonomy—to be in charge of our own lives. The tension between these opposing needs creates stress in human relationships. We want to enjoy the companionship of marriage without being required to get along with our spouse. We need friendship but find human relationships messy and problematic. As one introvert told me, "I like people, I just don't like to be with them." This human quandary has been going on for centuries, but it wasn't until recently that an innovation arose that promises to solve it. We call it social media.

Social Media

In 1996, Andrew Weinreich founded a small company built upon the assumption that any two people on earth are only six or fewer acquaintance links apart. Their website was called Six Degrees[1] and it was designed to connect unacquainted people electronically. Users created a profile and then attempted to "friend" other users and develop new relationships. It was in business until 2001 and is considered the first social media site.

Initial social media growth was slow, since relatively few people were connected to the Internet in the late 1990's. But as the Internet infrastructure expanded and people began to grasp its potential, other social media sites quickly appeared. Today almost anywhere on the globe people recognize the Facebook logo. Researchers tell us that an average user is spending around fifty minutes a day on social media. Over an American's average lifetime, this is five years spent connecting electronically.[2] Reports like this are concerning to many secular researchers, and one of them is author Sherry Turkle.

Turkle is a professor at the Massachusetts Institute of Technology. She has written several books assessing the effects of rapidly advancing technology on social behavior and human interaction. In her book *Alone Together* she writes, "We are lonely but fearful of intimacy."[3] Turkle explains how social media promises to give us the best of both worlds. Like the fabled Goldilocks, we want relationships that are not too close (that's uncomfortable), and not too far away (that's too lonely), but just right. Sites like Facebook provide this. If someone gets too distant, you can "unfriend" them. If someone starts to get too close, they can be ignored. Turkle says, "The world is now full of modern Goldilockses, people who take comfort in being in touch with a lot of people whom they can also keep at bay."[4]

Social media promises a wonderful answer to a centuries-old problem. Now we can be in control of our relationships and meet our relational needs without commitment or discomfort. Being physically present brings difficulties. We want to be with people, so we invite them over. But after a while we are ready for them to go home, and they don't always go when we are ready for them to. Or they ask personal questions that make us uncomfortable, and we wish that discussion could stop. Be honest. Haven't there been times when you would have liked to push a button and end an interaction? With social media, you are always just a click away from distancing yourself from a wearisome relationship.

Present but Not There

Healthy, vibrant relationships require time, effort, and maintenance. Humans aren't capable of simultaneously maintaining strong relationships with a large number of people. We are hindered by the confines of time and space. Even Jesus, with all His relational ability, restricted Himself to a small group of men. It could be argued that He only had a dozen close friends, and of those only three intimate friends. When I choose to interact with one person, I am choosing to exclude interaction with everyone else for the moment. As I talk with him face to face, I focus on what he is saying, connect with his life, and concentrate on relating to him. There are exceptions, and all of us find our minds wandering sometimes as we listen. But there is a certain inherent accountability that comes with face-to-face communication that doesn't allow us to stray too far.

Social media promises to override this uncomfortable confinement. Now you can be with someone physically while being with others virtually. We are no longer confined to relating to just one person at a time, and this ability can be intoxicating.

Recently we were in a restaurant, and across the aisle was a family with four children. I assume they had chosen to pause their hectic schedule and spend an evening together as a family. But each was focused on his own personal device. Occasionally one of them would chuckle, make a comment to the others, and then return to swiping his screen. They were physically present but mentally elsewhere.

Once again, it is secular researchers who are raising an alarm. In study after study, they are finding that we are losing more than we are gaining with technology. Not only do we lack the capability to multitask well, our thinking process is also being affected by this constant state of distraction. As noted in the book *Distracted*, "This is why we are less and less able to see, hear, and comprehend what's relevant and permanent, why so many of us feel that we can barely keep our heads above water, and our days are marked by perpetual loose ends."[5]

False Promises

In July 2017 the *American Journal of Preventative Medicine* published the results of a study conducted by the University of Pittsburgh. The report was titled "Association between Social Media Use and Depression among U.S. Young Adults."[6] They found that people who reported spending more than two hours a day on social media had twice the odds of feeling lonely compared to those who spent less than thirty minutes a day on these sites. Those who visited social media sites most frequently, fifty-eight visits a week or more, had more than three times the odds of loneliness than those who visited fewer than nine times a week. The results of this study came as a shock to many. After all, who could be more connected than those who are constantly connecting?

While there may be many reasons for these results, one fact seems clear: Social media isn't living up to its promises. When increased usage results in more loneliness and even depression, we should back up and ask why we're using it.

Why Isn't My Life Like That?

When people post life experiences on their social media page, they don't tend to share their mundane moments. They may have only gone bungee jumping once in the past two years, but if that is what you see when visiting their page, you subconsciously assume that bungee jumping represents their life. And as you scroll from page to page observing "friends" laughing in a group, purchasing new cars, and enjoying themselves on vacation, it is easy to assume that they are all out living the good life. You shut off your device and can't help wondering, "Am I the only one who is living a dull life?" You certainly don't want your friends to think so. The solution is plain. Take some exciting pictures and post them as soon as possible. Of course, you're not thinking about the fact that your "friends" are struggling with the same emotions, and your exciting pictures could further discourage them.

In 2013 a German study stated: "The wealth of social information presented on Facebook is astounding. While these affordances allow users to keep up to date, they also produce a basis for social comparison and envy on an unprecedented scale."[7] As followers of Jesus, do we really want to be involved in social platforms that encourage envy and social comparison? We should be extremely cautious in using anything that even secular researchers say can destroy our contentment. This isn't to say there are no good reasons to use social media. I have personally seen ways it is being used to bless the persecuted church. But we should be cautious for several reasons.

False Satisfaction

All of us are familiar with physical hunger. A few hours after breakfast something begins to gnaw deep inside. We know the solution for this inner discomfort: food! Our bodies need healthy nourishment to survive, and hunger is God's warning system telling us it is time to refuel. But appetites can be falsely satisfied. Just a piece of candy or some other sugary snack can mislead my body and make it believe, for short time, that my needs have been met and my body properly nourished.

God has also given us a hunger for relationship, and when a person hasn't been around others for a while, that hunger can grow intense. Before cell phones, we used to joke about long distance truckers and their reputation for talking. These men were on the road hour after hour without any human interaction. When they finally found another human, whether in a coffee shop or at a church function, they didn't let that person go until their relational appetite had been filled. Total isolation from other humans over long periods of time is almost unbearable. This is why prisons use solitary confinement as punishment. Granted, some people need more interaction than others, but all of us reach a point where our need has been quenched, and we are ready to be alone again. That is how God designed us.

Just as our hunger for physical nourishment can be falsely satisfied, so can our relational appetite. That normal need for relationship begins to gnaw deep inside, and out comes our electronic device. Time is spent virtually "connecting" with some friends, checking on news, and that need for relationship is eased. But before long, those pangs return and the cycle repeats itself. When this occurs, you are falsely satisfying your inner need for healthy dialogue and relationship with virtual interaction—relational candy. Keeping up with friends online can create a false sense of intimacy and temporarily quench that inner desire for face to face interaction. It can also squelch the God-given desire for significance and a meaningful life. But pseudo-relationships don't just fail to fulfill our needs. They also affect our ability to maintain real and vital relationships.

Virtual Excitement

There are reasons people spend hours staring at a little screen instead of fully engaging with daily life around them. Electronic reality provides stimulation that real life can hardly compete with. Mesmerizing motion, attention-grabbing graphics, and exciting sound effects are all calculated to captivate your attention. If real life could be more exciting and fulfilling than virtual programs, no one would bother to swipe the screen or search for a place to recharge the device. Videos from friends, movies, and social media interaction must, of necessity, be more stimulating than reality.

So what happens when the device is turned off? We must start interacting with real people, and real people now have become boring and difficult to understand. As a result, heavy users lose their appetite for real relationships—actual people can't compete. Shane Hipps describes it like this: "Digital social networking inoculates people against the desire to be physically present with others in real social networks—networks like a church or a meal at someone's home. Being together becomes nice but nonessential."[8]

Vital Human Relationships

In the last chapter we looked at ways electronic technology is threatening our relationship with God. But we must remember that healthy human relationships are also vital. Jesus told His followers to love their neighbors, and immediately a lawyer in the crowd wanted more explanation.[a] Why was this lawyer asking for parameters? Because he knew, as all of us know, that loving and relating to neighbors is messy business. They don't always act like we wish they would, say the things we would like, or ask convenient questions. But God made us for real relationships, and when we fall for cheap substitutes, we are striking an ax at the root of who God has called us to be. It may be tempting to pursue hundreds of virtual friends—who require nothing of you—rather than physically spending time with the neighbor next door. But don't fall for it. When we allow Satan to fill us and fool us with pseudo-reality, we are messing with something vital that God has placed within us.

---

[a] Luke 10:25–37

CHAPTER TEN

MEDIA MATTERS

In 1964 *Understanding Media* by Marshall McLuhan was published, and the very first sentence ended with the words "the medium is the message."[1] This little phrase stuck, and even though McLuhan had never used email, heard of an iPad, or engaged in social media, he was clearly on to something important. At the time, his message was controversial, but it is becoming increasingly relevant. We are being impacted not only by the messages received each day, but also by the various mediums used to receive them.

Whether I read my Bible on a printed page, an electronic tablet, or my phone, I'm receiving the same information, and it is easy to assume that the message is all that matters. But Marshall McLuhan disagrees. When we change the medium, our mind receives the message differently. To better understand, let's look at some different

> When we change the medium, our mind receives the message differently.

67

ways God has communicated with humanity in the past and consider how His methods for transmission affected the message.

When God Speaks . . .

After escaping through the Red Sea, the Hebrews were traveling through the wilderness, and God began a dialogue with Moses. He wanted to give the people His law, and He called Moses to the top of Mount Sinai to receive it. Notice how God asked Moses to come up.

> And Moses brought forth the people out of the camp to meet with God; and they stood at the nether part of the mount. [18]And Mount Sinai was altogether on a smoke, because the LORD descended upon it in fire: and the smoke thereof ascended as the smoke of a furnace, and the whole mount quaked greatly. [19]And when the voice of the trumpet sounded long, and waxed louder and louder, Moses spake, and God answered him by a voice. [20]And the LORD came down upon Mount Sinai, on the top of the mount: and the LORD called Moses up to the top of the mount; and Moses went up.[a]

What was the message? "Come up the mountain; I want to give the law to you." The medium? Fire and smoke, an earthquake, and a tremendous trumpet blast! It seems like an elaborate medium to carry such a little message. But God was not only telling Moses to come up—He was also telling the people who He is. They got the message through the medium. Notice a few verses later after Moses had given them God's commandments.

> And all the people saw the thunderings, and the lightnings, and the noise of the trumpet, and the mountain smoking: and when the people saw it, they

---
[a] Exodus 19:17–20

removed, and stood afar off. ¹⁹And they said unto Moses, Speak thou with us, and we will hear: but let not God speak with us, lest we die.[b]

These people had just received a message from God, but their minds were still on the medium, which conveyed a grandeur and awesomeness that gave force to the message.

Consider the medium of the Ten Commandments. These words, so familiar to us, were originally cut into stone.[c] Picture the long line of people waiting their turn to view these words. Imagine their thoughts as they viewed these words carved into solid stone. The message is the same one we read in our Bibles on paper, but the medium of stone gave perspective and a stronger impact. This was an ageless and unchanging God who obviously meant what He said!

The Electronic Page

So how do different mediums affect us? Although the difference is not always huge, studies have consistently shown that we retain less when reading from a screen than from the printed page.[2] There are several reasons for this, and one is the presence of hypertext.

Hypertext is usually highlighted or underlined, and clicking or tapping on it leads to other articles or information regarding the topic at hand. This can help you explore the subject in more detail, but it can also distract you from seeing the larger message. As one tech writer has noted, "Because it disrupts concentration, such activity weakens comprehension."[3] This doesn't mean one shouldn't use media that contains hypertext. Indeed, you can't escape hypertext if you plan to read information online. Just being aware of its ability to distract can help us to ignore it.

Hypertext isn't the only thing lowering our comprehension and retention. Nicholas Carr observes: "The shift from paper to screen doesn't just change the way we navigate a piece of writing. It also

---

[b] Exodus 20:18, 19

[c] Deuteronomy 4

influences the degree of attention we devote to it and the depth of our immersion in it."[4] I enjoy using electronic readers, especially on long trips where the alternative is lugging multiple books through airports. So of course I am concerned when I read this kind of research.

As I try to understand the "why" behind the research, one common denominator keeps appearing. It seems that the more "life" there is in the medium, the less our brains feel the need to be involved. In 2014 a study found that "readers using Kindles were less competent in recalling the plot and events in the book than those who used paperbacks."[5] This statistic is even more disturbing since Kindles resemble paper books more than many other devices used today.

We are affected not only by words, but also by how these words are presented. Colors, print fonts, the devices we use—all of these shape how our brains receive information. Think about chiseling words into stone tablets centuries ago. Think about Christians printing Bibles in restricted countries today. Does the effort behind the print or the great risk someone took to produce it affect how a book is read? Absolutely!

The Price of the Medium

A few years ago I visited a home in Romania where Bibles had been printed during the Communist era. The older people living there still remember the great risk many took. Those Bibles were printed in an attic, with mattresses lining the walls to dampen the noise. The printers knew full well that torture awaited if they were discovered. Imagine receiving a Bible from one of these presses. What if you knew that someone was being tortured so that you could have a Bible? How might that affect the way you read and receive the message? The words would be the same, but imagine how that knowledge might add force to the message.

We live in an era inflated with information. Printed material, electronic communication, advertisements, news feeds, billboards, newspapers—all attempt to transfer messages to our minds. Amid this informational deluge, I find myself devaluing the printed word. Emails and printed material have to be dealt with and disposed of. When I sit down to read my Bible, I sometimes find it difficult to give the words I am reading proper weight and focus. This is a dangerous posture to have toward the Word of God.

The Apostle Paul told Timothy, "All scripture is given by inspiration of God, and is profitable for doctrine, for reproof, for correction, for instruction in righteousness: That the man of God may be perfect, throughly furnished unto all good works."[d] We are to seek God through His Word, not just because reading the Bible is what all good Christians do, but to prepare for action. And part of that action is becoming the medium that takes the message to others.

We Are the Medium

Jesus came to the world to show us the Father.[e] His speech pointed men to His Father, while His actions demonstrated His Father's character.[f] Jesus' life was without sin,[g] He went about doing good,[h] and the motive behind every action was to please His Father.[i] This is why Jesus Christ was the perfect medium for the message.

Before He left, Jesus transferred to His followers the mission of demonstrating the Father to the world. "As my Father hath sent me, even so send I you," He told his disciples.[j] Paul had to remind the church of Corinth of this responsibility. He told them they were to be epistles, "known and read of all men."[k] God has always desired to communicate reconciliation to a lost world. The believers are the medium carrying this message, and now it is our opportunity. How we live our daily lives impacts the message.

---

[d] 2 Timothy 3:16, 17
[e] John 14:9
[f] Hebrews 1:3
[g] 2 Corinthians 5:21
[h] Acts 10:38
[i] John 8:29
[j] John 20:21
[k] 2 Corinthians 3:2

CHAPTER ELEVEN

A SOUND-BITE SOCIETY

During a recent trip to town my wife overheard two older women discussing the need for their grandchildren to plan for their futures. One had a grandson who would soon graduate from high school but wasn't very interested in furthering his education. He explained his position by saying, "I don't need to go to college, Grandma. I have Google!" Why go to the expense of college, sit through years of classes, study textbooks, and submit to grueling tests, when everything he needs to know about any subject is readily available online?

> "I don't need to go to college, Grandma. I have Google!"

This argument sounds plausible until you ponder potential outcomes. How would you feel about boarding an airliner only to discover that your pilot had never actually flown a plane? Instead, he assures you, he has spent many hours on YouTube learning how to fly. Would you be comfortable staying on that flight? Of course not! Information is essential, but we want the people flying the plane to have much more than just knowledge.

Knowledge versus Wisdom

There is a growing assumption in our culture that the accumulation of knowledge is our primary need. This supposition comes from many sources, including the leaders within the tech industry itself. Sergey Brin, one of Google's founders, said, "Certainly if you had all the world's information directly attached to your brain, or an artificial brain that was smarter than your brain, you'd be better off."[1] This statement reflects a basic assumption: Life would be better if we all had more information. Google is trying to achieve this goal. While many of us benefit by using the Internet for research, is more knowledge really our greatest need? What is knowledge, and how does it differ from wisdom?

Knowledge, put simply, is an accumulation of facts or information gained through experience or education. I want the man holding the scalpel while I am on the surgery table to have lots of knowledge. But I also want him to possess wisdom.

Wisdom is understanding how to use knowledge in an intelligent way. It is the ability to sift through the available facts, make a judgment call, and apply the information correctly to the situation at hand. Consequently, as the amount of information increases, so does the need for wisdom to decide what is true and useful, and what should be discarded. With technology, we can instantly connect with more facts than ever before. But do we have the wisdom to discern what is true and useful? Are we prepared to sift through all the information and separate truth from error? The more available knowledge, the greater the need for wisdom.

Respect for Age

People who have lived longer have more experience, more knowledge of how life works, and much wisdom to share with youth. Historically, old men were revered, and younger men viewed as less important. This is why the Apostle Paul told Timothy, "Let no man despise thy youth."[a] Today, if something goes wrong with my computer or some electronic gadget, I find myself seeking out someone who is younger. Most leaders in this electronic explosion are relatively young men. Those providing the capital may be older, but the thinkers and the electronic heroes of our time are young. This influences the way society views age and experience. Much of the focus is on young people, and I contend that technology, along with valuing information over wisdom, has assisted this cultural shift. Products, services, and ease of lifestyle keep improving, and our society has its eyes on the future. Consequently, older generations and the lessons of the past are valued less and less.

Confirming My Opinion

I have observed an alarming fact about myself. I love to discover stories or articles that confirm what I already believe. And when I find writings that agree with my opinion, I rarely investigate their validity. On the other hand, if I read something that disagrees with my opinion, I am immediately suspicious. How do I know it's true? Did the author really do his research? I thoroughly investigate such writing, all the while suspecting it contains falsehood. If I look long enough, I can find evidence that validates my opinion and proves the suspicious account incorrect.

This tendency is as old as human history, but the Internet has compounded the problem. Let's assume I believe global warming is a viable and dangerous threat to the planet, yet occasionally I run across some right-wing information that disagrees. Since Google is designed to give me the information I want, the disagreeable "facts" can quickly be debunked. Or let's say I believe global warming is a lie promoted by those liberal lefties. Once again, I can go to the Internet and disprove the information. Is this the Internet's fault? No, but quick access to so much information makes it easy to follow my natural tendency to investigate and disprove what I disagree with.

---

[a] 1 Timothy 4:12

It gets worse. Each time you choose a website, your choice runs through an online algorithm. The next time you search a similar topic, the odds increase that similar information will appear. Over time, your searches will increasingly produce results that agree with your point of view. The man who believes in global warming, for example, will increasingly see articles agreeing with his point of view, and the man who believes it is a scam will also become more established in his view. Some refer to this as an echo chamber, a place where each person keeps "hearing" the same point of view over and over again. In an article titled "The Reason Your Feed Became an Echo Chamber" one writer said, "Algorithms . . . steer us toward articles that reflect our own ideological preferences, and search results usually echo what we already know and like. As a result, we aren't exposed to other ideas and viewpoints."[2]

We are seeing the results of this in our culture. People on different sides of many issues can't understand why the opposition can't see truth. All sides are doing their research, but over time the "facts" they discover do not agree. They assume the others aren't interested in truth, and animosity among them grows. It is difficult to bring people together who receive different results when searching the same issue.

False Confidence

Access to virtually unlimited information, a ready answer for any question, and constant exposure to facts that agree with your opinion—this is a recipe for false confidence. As the young man who snubbed college illustrates, we assume we have sufficient information and little need for additional learning or alternate viewpoints. Pride and overconfidence existed long before the Internet, but I believe we underestimate how it compounds our arrogant tendencies.

In the past, when facing a difficult issue, people tended to ask the wise elders in their community. Vigorous discussions occurred around the dinner table, and issues were deliberated from differing perspectives. But why spend time wrestling when instant answers are always within reach? We want information and we want it fast. Consequently, we shortcut a vital process—deep thinking.

A Shallow Society

The instant access to information puts us at risk of losing our desire and ability to think deeply. When a culture loses its ability to think deeply on important issues, it has lost something of vital importance. We are seeing the results of shallow thinking on every front.

Modern life demands that we process an incredible amount of information on a multitude of topics every day. There is so much to sift and process that we find ourselves going through our tasks with frenzied urgency. How do we know what is essential and what is unneeded? We glance over news reports, scan emails, and skim printed material, all while dealing with constant interruptions from our phones. We hurriedly attempt to garner the crucial information amid distractions. Like a flat stone skipping across a lake, we try to grasp some news about this issue, respond to that situation, and listen to this problem, all while carrying on with our daily lives. The result is that we know a little about a lot of things, but we no longer feel the need to think deeply or retain information.

In a 2006 poll, it was discovered that 60 percent of young adults in America were unable to locate Iraq on a map.[3] The United States had been at war with them for three years, and every night information about the war, including maps of the country, had flashed across television screens. Despite all this exposure to fact, little geographical information had been retained. Technology's ability to flood us with information subconsciously assures us there is little reason to retain or reflect. After all, tomorrow will bring another flood of information, so why ponder or retain the facts confronting us today? If we need to know where Iraq is, we can always Google it. This subconscious reliance on technology is changing not only how we think, but whether we think at all.

Shorter Attention Span

Pick up any book written over one hundred years ago and notice the length of sentences. Or just start counting words within sentences in the Apostle Paul's writings, and you will notice that something has changed dramatically. Sentences today are much shorter. We no longer have the patience for long rambling descriptive sentences.[b] After all, we have more information we want to explore, and we can't afford to wade through long sentences. But another possibility concerns me. As I read some of these older writings, the sentences are so lengthy that I struggle to retain thoughts from the first part of the sentence and connect them with the conclusion. Is it possible that constant use of technology and the flood of information is affecting my memory and thought processes?

> This subconscious reliance on technology is changing not only how we think, but whether we think at all.

A few years ago I visited an inner city mission. They were reaching out to children between eight and twelve years old who, tired of sitting at home watching television or roaming the streets, came to enjoy some wholesome games, Biblical teaching, and snacks. I had been asked to share a short devotional, but a few minutes into my presentation I noticed something. When I told an exciting story, I had their attention. But as soon as I shifted to applying the moral of the story, their eyes began to wander. I had lost them. To woo them back, I would add more emphasis and drama. Once again when the captivating story concluded, their attention was gone.

Suddenly it occurred to me what was happening. I was competing

---

[b] The length of sentences was dropping long before the internet. In 1892, Edwin Lewis wrote a book titled *History of the English Paragraph*. In it he stated: "The English sentence has decreased in average length at least one half in three hundred years." Five hundred years ago the average sentence contained sixty-one words. Today sentences range from fifteen to twenty words." —<https://medium.com/@theacropolitan/sentence-length-has-declined-75-in-the-past-500-years-2e40f80f589f>, accessed on December 20, 2018.

with television! These children had been raised with a piece of technology designed to captivate. "Normal" for them was completely out of my reach as a speaker. From a young age, they had been fed short bursts of stimuli, and they had lost their ability to listen to a story, ponder its meaning, and apply it to real life. Their attention spans were just too short! I left that night with great sadness. Constant exposure to fast-paced stimuli had robbed them of their ability to think as God intended.

Is it possible that we are falling prey to the same peril? Today we have decided that shorter is better. By rushing through each day, we are shunning not only long sentences, but also long books and long sermons. We are increasingly drawn to authors and speakers who are concise and entertaining. Where at one time listening to and meditating on preaching from the Word of God was enough, now speakers feel pressured to use object lessons, whiteboards, PowerPoint, or other techniques to ensure their listeners are sufficiently engaged. While there is nothing wrong with these tools, this constant need for visual stimuli points to a deeper issue.

Increasingly we avoid big books with deep theology, preferring lighter, shorter, and more enjoyable reads. We like study guides, life application Bibles, and fifteen-minute devotionals. Let someone else do the difficult study. We prefer easy-to-digest material that we can grab on the run.

What will be the long-term effect of this on the church? Where are the young people in this generation who are willing to turn their gadgets off for a while and think deeply? Youth who take the time to slowly go through the Word of God, prayerfully ponder its teaching, and meditate on where God may be calling us today? Who will have enough time to carefully analyze the lessons from church history? What will be the result of churches full of people too busy to spend time in prayer and fasting, or more enamored with cute sound bites than the still, small voice of God?

CHAPTER TWELVE

BRAIN CHANGE

No part of the body is more amazing and mysterious than the human brain. Set inside a rigid case of bone, it exists in total darkness while floating in cerebrospinal fluid designed to insulate and protect. For centuries men speculated and debated about this extraordinary organ, hypothesizing the location where mental processes and memory occurred. Visitors in London can still see Leonardo da Vinci's drawings from the early 1500s as he attempted to depict brain functions.

Many of da Vinci's drawings were based on dissected ox brains. His successor, Andreas Vesalius, would plead with executioners for recently decapitated heads, dissect them while they were still warm from the execution, and then make drawings.[1] His goal was to show what the brain looks like and to trace specific nerves that transferred information to figure out how this amazing and mysterious organ works.

Even though research on the brain has come a long way, men are still awed by the brain's capabilities. How can this lump of gray matter process my thoughts, contain all my memories, and give direction to every part of my body? How can a three-pound blob (surgeons tell us it has the consistency of cream cheese) contain my personality? Is it possible that my character, that part of me that makes me unique from any other person, is suspended and resides somewhere in this little mass of blood vessels, tissue, and cellular structure? Amazing!

Some incredible things go on inside this lump of matter, and researchers continually discover that the brain is far more complex than anyone ever imagined.[a] Perhaps even more remarkable and pertinent to our subject of technology, they have also learned that the brain isn't static. In fact, it in is in a constant state of change, continuously rewiring and altering itself as you use it each day!

My Brain Is Changing?

For centuries it was assumed that an adult's brain was similar to mechanical contraptions. A steam or gas engine has many moving parts, and each fulfills a specific function. Doctors assumed the brain and nervous system were the same. Just as a piston in an engine cannot suddenly decide to be a tire, they believed sections of the brain were locked into particular functions. In recent years this view has been challenged. One of the men leading this research is a neuroscientist named Michael Merzenich.

In 1968 Merzenich was working on a brain-mapping project at the University of Wisconsin. He had removed a portion of skull from several monkeys and begun mapping sections of their brains using a hair-thin electronic probe. Finding the approximate location that registers sensations from the monkey's hand, he would touch the hand until the neurons beside the tip of his probe fired. By doing this thousands of times, he developed a map showing in minute detail exactly where the monkey processed what its hand was feeling. Merzenich did this on six monkeys, and then moved

---

[a] Neuroscientist Roger Sperry wrote, "In the human head there are forces within forces within forces, as in no other cubic half-foot of the universe we know." —Walsh and Bolen, *The Neurobiology of Human Behavior*, p. 1.

on to his next experiment.

He made small cuts on each monkey's hands with a scalpel, severing sensory nerves. His goal was to discover how the brain responds when a nerve is damaged and then allowed to heal. Merzenich continued to monitor these monkeys over the next few days, and, as expected, the damaged nerves grew back in a haphazard fashion and the brain became confused. For example, when he touched the lower part of a finger the monkey's brain registered that the sensation was coming from the tip. Communication had been mixed up and the brain's map scrambled.

A surprise came several months later. When Merzenich went back and conducted the same experiment, this initial mix-up was repaired. Merzenich was startled. The monkeys' brains had reorganized themselves. Today, the brain's ability to restructure itself is known as neuroplasticity, but at the time this discovery flew in the face of conventional wisdom. "Looking back on it, I realized that I had seen evidence of neuroplasticity. But I didn't know it at the time. I simply didn't know what I was seeing. And besides, in mainstream neuroscience, nobody would believe that plasticity was occurring on this scale."[2]

Neuroplasticity

Researchers are discovering how "plastic" our brains really are. It was once believed that our brains are hardwired at a young age and change very little as adults, but now scientists are discovering that our minds are constantly rewiring themselves. Our brain neurons are continually breaking old connections and creating new ones. In addition, as we learn new things, new nerve cells are being formed. Our brains have been designed to expand as they learn.

Other than God's initial hardwiring, we come into this world with zero knowledge. At birth, our brains are immediately assailed with massive amounts of input. Sounds, feelings, tastes, smells—a tremendous amount of information comes crashing into our brains. Initially it is just a tangled chaos of data. Look into the face of a newborn child and you'll see a certain blankness in her eyes. So much information is flowing in and she is simply trying to make sense of what is occurring. But it isn't long till the brain begins to sort through this information. The child starts to recognize voices and faces, and her mind begins to decide which sights and sounds are important and which can be discarded.

When we execute a task or experience a sensation, a specific set of neurons is activated. As this is repeated, the connection between these neurons, called synaptic links, is strengthened. Over time, as processes are repeated over and over, these pathways of neurons become established and grow stronger. What researchers are discovering is that this process doesn't cease as we move into adulthood. As we get older, our environment and our choices create new pathways. Each time we perform an action or engage in a thought, we are making it easier to do it again. As one author has said, "The chains of linked neurons form our minds' true vital paths."[3] In other words, every thought is influencing future ones.

Vital Pathways

The implications of this should be sobering. When I choose to respond to my wife in a negative way, I am doing more than just escalating tension in our relationship. I am also making it easier to repeat that response in the future. Every type of mental activity I engage in is actually reprogramming my brain. This can be a blessing. As I type right now, I don't need to give much conscious thought to which key to hit. I have engaged in this activity enough that pathways in my mind transfer a thought to a keystroke almost immediately. But it also points out the importance of reviewing my daily choices and guarding these vital pathways that I am constantly creating or strengthening. It also calls for a closer look at how technology is impacting these pathways.

Gary Small, a professor of psychiatry at UCLA, is one of many researchers today sounding an alarm. According to him, "The current explosion of digital technology not only is changing the way we live and communicate, but is rapidly and profoundly altering our brains."[4] This easy access to a massive amount of information, coupled with constant distraction, is reprograming and rewiring our thought processes. While these tools provide accessibility to a wealth of valuable information, this technology can change our ability to process data in ways we don't yet fully understand.

As I have tried to comprehend the fears expressed by secular researchers, there are several additional concerns that I believe followers of Jesus should carefully consider.

Clicking More, Thinking Less

Recently I was purchasing a fifty-cent item; I handed the girl at the cash register a dollar bill. She promptly hit the appropriate keys and then looked at the display to determine how much change to return. All of us have been there. We grow so accustomed to electronic tools, whether calculators, smartphones, or computers, that we fail to process the smallest of calculations. After all, it is so much easier to just do what the display tells us. But what is this doing to these vital pathways in our brain? Mental calculations strengthen our ability to think. Each time we avoid these processes, our ability to calculate grows weaker. What will be the long-term effect of this shift? What about the constant use of electronic concordances? It is so easy, but are we losing our ability to remember the location of familiar passages?

Linear Thought

One of my challenges when traveling in foreign countries is language. I listen to two natives conversing and I want so badly to understand their discussion. If it is a country I have visited several times, I can pick up occasional words, so I try to link them and determine what is being said. Sometimes I can put it together, but often I am completely off base. This is simply because I have a fragmented view of the conversation. When you thoroughly understand a language and use it in real life, you employ linear thinking.

Linear thinking is the ability to take pieces of information about a subject and put them into a logical sequence so they can be useful. It is one thing to accumulate a mountain of facts. It is entirely another to have the ability, wisdom, and experience to link these fragmented facts and make them useful.

> It is one thing to accumulate a mountain of facts. It is entirely another to link these fragmented facts and make them useful.

If I want to learn about heart surgery, for example, I can Google questions and instantly have answers. If I continue doing this, I can amass much knowledge about heart surgery. But despite my feeling of accomplishment, all I have done is assemble facts on the subject. You would be very skeptical about crawling up on the operating table with me wielding a knife. Why?

Despite the vast amount of knowledge I have assembled, I am unprepared for surgery. I don't have the experience to know what I don't know or even to know which "facts" are correct. If you need heart surgery, you want a cardiologist who has demonstrated repeatedly that he can pair knowledge with wisdom and expertise. This is one of the challenges that technology brings. Piles of knowledge, and false confidence. Information must be interpreted and evaluated to be useful, and this was a huge hurdle when the internet first appeared.[b] Even though the search engines today make sorting information much easier, this challenge still exists. It is easy to believe that we have wisdom, when in reality we only have access to a huge pile of fragments.

---

[b] In a 1995 Newsweek article on the problems with the Internet, Clifford Stoll wrote, "What the Internet hucksters won't tell you is that the Internet is one big ocean of unedited data, without any pretense of completeness. Lacking editors, reviewers or critics, the Internet has become a wasteland of unfiltered data. You don't know what to ignore and what's worth reading." —Clifford Stoll, "Why the Web Won't Be Nirvana," *Newsweek*, February 26, 1995. Newer search engines try to filter, but just because something is on the Internet does not assure its validity. —GM

Loss of Lasting Memory

Knowledge is intended to be a building process. "For precept must be upon precept, precept upon precept," the prophet Isaiah wrote many years ago, "line upon line, line upon line; here a little, and there a little."[c] It takes time for facts to embed themselves in long-term memory, and researchers today are validating this Biblical truth.[d] Even though we go through a prodigious amount of information every day, we retain little of it. Neurologists say this is a result of failing to attend, or to take the time to think deeply. We must connect information to what we already know for it to become entrenched and useful. Technology promises to deliver faster results, but unfortunately, it is difficult to retain information that requires little effort to acquire.

As I read the concerns of secular researchers regarding how technology is altering our ability to think deeply, I wonder. Shouldn't passionate pursuers of God be even more concerned than the secular world? I am thankful that many are taking this challenge seriously, but there is much to be done. Technology capable of shaping our minds and creating shallow reasoning should be viewed with extreme caution.[e]

Men have a God-given desire to improve. Whether a man believes in God or not, when he invents something, he is demonstrating a characteristic of God Himself. Whether it is a farmer transforming wasteland into a productive field, a remodeler renovating a deserted house, or a developer improving a piece of software, when we transform chaos into orderliness, we are demonstrating the image of the Creator. Men may deny God's involvement and say He doesn't exist,

---

[c] Isaiah 28:10

[d] Neuroscientist Eric Kandel explains it like this: "For a memory to persist, the incoming information must be thoroughly and deeply processed. This is accomplished by attending to the information and associating it meaningfully and systematically with knowledge already well established in memory." —Kandel, *In Search of Memory*, p. 210.

[e] Nicholas Carr writes, "The Net may well be the most mind-altering technology that has ever come into general use. At the very least, it's the most powerful that has come along since the book." —*The Shallows: What the Internet Is Doing to Our Brains*, p. 116.

yet each time they find better ways to do things or make improvements, they portray the image of the One they deny.

God intends for us to use the minds He has given us. But it is time we stop and ask ourselves some difficult questions. Is easier always better? In our attempt to do something faster, are we losing something else of greater value—something with spiritual consequences?

PART THREE 3

DEADLY DIVERSIONS

CHAPTER THIRTEEN

DIGITAL DISTRACTIONS

It was 2012, and I was sitting in the kitchen of a middle-class Romanian family. Across from me were two men, a grandfather and his son, who had agreed to share a little about their lives. These men had firsthand exposure to physical persecution for their faith. They knew what it was like to gather in secret, to look over their shoulders during a baptism, to see Christian brothers and sisters hauled off by the Romanian secret police to the torture chamber.

The grandfather, Mihai, was born in 1927, and at eighty-five years of age he had many experiences to share. He described in a shaky voice what it was like growing up in a Romanian Orthodox home with little knowledge about Jesus. There were a few small evangelical churches in the area, but Mihai knew attending one of these was off limits. Yet he was curious. Why would people choose to join these churches, knowing they would be persecuted by the local Orthodox Church and the community? Mihai's curiosity grew. One evening in 1949, at age twenty-two, he decided to investigate.

On New Year's Eve Mihai was walking through town and heard singing as he passed one of these little churches. Looking both ways, he slipped inside, and for the first time heard the saving message of Jesus Christ. He learned of his own sin and the provision available through God's grace, and that night Mihai found salvation through Jesus Christ. He walked out the door rejoicing in his new faith. He had found what his soul longed for.

In the coming days he also found out something else. Mihai discovered that "all those who live godly in Christ Jesus shall suffer persecution."[a] He learned what it was like to be shunned by neighbors and family. But difficult as those first years were, more severe trials were ahead.

Coming of Communism

Four years after his decision to follow Jesus, Mihai was married and had welcomed a son, Marcel, into his family. It was a time of great political upheaval in Romania. The communist government was nationalizing private companies and setting up collective farms. Then in 1965 Nicolae Ceausescu came into power, and life in Romania began to change even more dramatically. Marcel was just twelve years old when Ceausescu began to exert his influence, and he shared what it was like growing up in these tumultuous years. While Mihai had dealt with opposition from the Orthodox Church, Marcel's religious oppression came from the government itself.

Ceausescu's Romania was a land of lies and brutality. Questioning a government policy could lead to imprisonment, torture, and in some situations, death. People lived in a continual state of anxiety and mistrust. Neighbors watched each other suspiciously. The government encouraged citizens to report any derogatory statements about the regime made by classmates, coworkers, or even family members. Spies were everywhere, and the way to survive was to remain silent and blend in.

The communist government was opposed to religious activities. Romanian citizens were expected to give their allegiance to the

---

[a] 2 Timothy 3:12

government alone, and Christians were frequently arrested, imprisoned, and persecuted. Marcel told of friends during these years who were detained and tortured for their faith. When they went to church services, they were aware that others from their congregation were imprisoned and abused. When Marcel decided to follow Jesus as a young man, he was aware of the danger. Yet he chose to take an even greater risk.

In 1979 twenty-six-year-old Marcel was asked if he would help with an extremely dangerous project. There was an attempt underway to get Bibles from Germany, across Europe, and into other parts of the Soviet Union to the East. The goal was to bring Bibles to various storage locations in central Romania and find local believers willing to transport them by car to the Moldovan border. There the Bibles would be dropped at a construction site where a dam was being built on the Prut River, loaded into dump trucks along with stones being used in the construction, and transported to the Moldovan side of the river. From there another team would take the Bibles to their final destination.

Marcel responded to this request. Night after night he loaded his Romanian-made Dacia full of Bibles, drove hundreds of kilometers to the dam to unload, returned home, and prepared to do it again. Marcel estimated he traveled around 19,000 kilometers each month during this project, and each trip was fraught with danger. Being caught with a carload of Bibles in those days was a ticket to prison and torture.

Great precautions were taken. Just one spy in this long chain of smugglers would endanger the entire network. Many faithful believers were involved, yet Marcel didn't even know who they were. It would be years before he was finally able to meet others in the network who had survived.

Marcel couldn't even read the Bibles he was carrying. They were Russian, intended for Christians in other areas. These men had nothing to gain personally by being involved. They were simply driven by a love for other believers, and willing to take great personal risk to bless them.

As I sat in this little Romanian kitchen, I was fascinated. Here were two men who had lived in times when persecution was an expected part of Christianity. Marcel had experienced the terror of watching a car he passed in the middle of the night make a U-turn and start following him. He knew what it was like to pray fervently, knowing that if this was the secret police, he was headed for torture.

But these two men were not alone at the kitchen table. A younger family member was listening, and his name was Paul.

Paul was nineteen years old, the son of Marcel and grandson of Mihai. Paul grew up listening to these stories. He had heard his father recount almost getting caught while smuggling Bibles. His father described the spiritual vibrancy that had existed during that time. Yet Paul's life in modern Romania has been completely different—so different that he has trouble relating.

"These stories are fascinating for my generation to hear. It's amazing! I love hearing how they smuggled Bibles, covering them with sand and stuff. But it is so different now. Bibles aren't treasured like that." Paul talked about his daily life and spiritual journey compared to his father and grandfather when they were his age. Paul was also honest about his own spiritual struggles. He would like to be closer to the Lord, but has difficulty finding time for personal devotions. When I inquired about his greatest obstacle, he didn't hesitate. "Technology."

Paul spends about six hours each day on his computer. He comes home from school and immediately gets online to check email, communicate with friends on social media, or play an online game. But his greatest challenge is movies.

"For me, movies are a problem. I know they are affecting my

spiritual life. Sometimes I try making promises, knowing I have to cut some of this out. They take a lot of my time." Paul seemed genuinely perplexed by his inability to overcome the lure of digital entertainment.

Three Men—Three Risks

Three men representing three generations. Each publicly confessed faith in Jesus, had a desire to serve his Lord, and experienced spiritual warfare. The first decided to follow Jesus at great risk. He swam against the prevailing religious current of his day, trusting his Lord for protection.

The second willingly also took great risk for the kingdom. He could have hunkered down, taught his own family, and ignored the spiritual needs of others. Instead, he chose to risk his life to expand the kingdom of God.

The third was at great risk of losing everything the previous two generations had fought for. By his own admission, he found technology a powerful and seductive force against spiritual growth. He confessed his lack of spiritual passion and longed for the faith and zeal he observed in his father and grandfather.

As I listened I couldn't help but wonder: Am I fully grasping the danger of our day? Imagine how much time these two older men must have spent praying and longing for relief from the communist regime with its persecution, limited access to Bibles, and daily atheist indoctrination for children. They longed to be free from the tyranny of oppression.

Yet both older men admitted that this present day of entertainment and constant digital distraction is more dangerous for youth than life under Ceausescu had been. In those days it was risky to attend prayer meetings, yet they were heavily attended. Today it is easy to go, but the number of meetings has been reduced because attendance is sparse. In the past, youth were told that God didn't exist, yet these older men couldn't think of any youth in their church who had walked away from God. Today there are plenty of Bibles and spiritual freedom, yet the church is finding it difficult to keep young people. No wonder Mihai and Marcel see our time as more dangerous than theirs!

While it would be unfair to blame all current spiritual lethargy on technology, it is time that we sit up and take notice. We underestimate the impact digital content is having, not just on our youth, but on all of us. Electronic technology is changing our occupations, our expectations, our capacity for patience, and our ability to think deeply. Consequently, it can change our churches. And perhaps the greatest danger of all is its ability to sidetrack us from the disciplines required for spiritual life. Young Paul in Romania is not alone. Many youths in conservative Christian churches are caught up in the speed and power of technology.

CHAPTER FOURTEEN

SEDUCED BY SIGHT AND SOUND

Delta Airlines Flight 0054, having left Atlanta about two hours ago, still has ten more hours till it is scheduled to land in Lagos, Nigeria. Sitting here in seat 12B, not quite drowsy enough to sleep, I pull out a book, trying to redeem the time. Long international flights can be tiring. Unbroken periods of sitting, inability to find a comfortable sleeping position, multiple time zones—all of this translates into physical exhaustion. But bodily fatigue isn't the only challenge. I am also being assaulted on another level.

Personal video players in each seatback are designed to ensure that no traveler is bored. Across the aisle in 12C a child is watching cartoons, the person in 11C is watching a scantily clad woman attempt to seduce a man on the screen, and my neighbor in 12A is playing Solitaire on her phone while keeping track of a motorcycle chase in a movie. The cyclist is jumping cars, shooting through flames, and achieving impossible feats to avoid his pursuer. Part of me is disgusted at the unrealistic scenes, yet I find myself drawn into the drama. I look back down at my book in a feeble attempt to engage with the text, but can't help wondering how this motorcycle chase will end. Can he keep up this frantic pace and elude his gun-toting pursuers?

I look back down at the page, tell myself that watching is a waste of time, and attempt to refocus. But what is happening now? Another quick glance, and the film has turned into a graphic display of extreme violence—men slaughtering each other, close-up pictures of bloody bodies. This time it isn't hard to look away. I am puzzled though. Earlier in the flight I had discussed spiritual views with the young woman beside me. She is a Nigerian Roman Catholic who claims to be following Jesus. How can she enjoy watching this carnage?

I turned to her. She popped her ear buds out, and I asked, "Do you really enjoy watching this kind of violence?"

She said she did. She knew it wasn't real, and she found the fast-paced action entertaining. We discussed this a little, and then I asked her, "Do you think Jesus would enjoy watching people slaughter each other?"

This time she paused a moment. "Yes, I think He would. Because our lives are a spiritual battle, and these movies reflect our spiritual lives."

Her answer stunned me. Jesus would enjoy watching people slaughter each other? The man who taught His followers to love their enemies would enjoy seeing bloody displays of vengeance? That obviously wasn't reasonable, but she was clearly convinced and eager to return to her movie.

As she reinserted her ear buds, I sat trying to comprehend the compelling power of the entertainment world.[a] My Roman Catholic seatmate seemed incapable of seeing how she had been ensnared. Looking back down at my book, I was struck by the irony of what I had been trying to read. It was Neil Postman's classic *Amusing Ourselves to Death*.

---

[a] Ben Franklin once said, "So convenient a thing it is to be a reasonable creature, since it enables one to find or make a reason for everything one has a mind to do." —<http://www.ushistory.org/franklin/autobiography/page18.htm>, accessed on August 9, 2017.

Video's Captivating Power

Neil Postman looked around at his culture and became alarmed. *Amusing Ourselves to Death* is a direct attack on modern culture's insatiable craving to be entertained. It also discusses how electronic sight and sound are having a powerful negative impact on democracy, education, and the local church. But the interesting feature of the book is its prophetic nature. Postman was perturbed at how rapidly video had changed his culture, yet his book was written in 1985, long before the iPad, iPhone, and other handheld devices. The book was a solemn warning about the devastating sway television had already had on the American people. Yet there was no way Postman could have anticipated what was to come.

In 1985 computers were simply huge data crunching devices. They churned through incredible amounts of information but took up entire rooms. Postman could not have dreamed of devices so small yet so fast and powerful that young people could, within the privacy of their bedrooms, send and receive videos that would have been illegal to broadcast on public networks in 1985. But he did warn that Americans would receive the growing use of computers and videos with "their customary mindless inattention; which means they will use it as they are told, without a whimper."[1]

Video's Productive Power

Recently I saw a young man watching a video on how to repair the door handle on a vehicle. The clip was a few minutes long, and it would have taken quite a bit of writing to deliver the same instructions. Whether repairing something, learning about another country, or watching a news report, there are many ways video is being used productively. It is one thing to read a report on a recent disaster, and quite another to experience the sights and sounds associated with the tragedy.

This morning I received an email with pictures and links informing me about a recent flood in Bangladesh. As I looked at the roaring water, the terrified expressions on children's faces, and the sight of bodies and buildings being propelled downstream in a rushing muddy river, I had to stop and reflect. How many words would it have taken to describe this catastrophe? How many paragraphs would it take to convey the devastation and terror you can observe in a thirty-second video clip? Video can be an amazing platform to transfer an incredible amount of useful information in a very short period.

Video's Deceptive Tendency

This capability to rapidly convey information also increases the ability to deceive. As our world moves away from print and toward video, I wonder if we understand video's destructive tendencies. I have heard intelligent adults propose that there is really no difference between receiving a message through electronic media versus receiving it through print. In other words, there is no difference between reading a book and watching the movie, or reading an advertisement about a product and watching a clip promoting it. That is foolishness. Failing to recognize the incredible power in video makes us much more susceptible to its deceptive power. Let's look closer at the difference between receiving information through print and image.

> Failing to recognize the incredible power in video makes us much more susceptible to its deceptive power.

Print versus Image

All of us are familiar with the saying, "A picture is worth a thousand words." A good picture can transfer an incredible amount of information in a brief time. Think of Norman Rockwell's artwork. How long would it take to describe everything that is going on in one of his paintings? His pictures can convey human longing, fear, and intense emotions in seconds. Witnessing these emotions in fellow humans moves and motivates us in ways that are almost impossible to do with plain text. The advertisement industry understands that images impact people. While text primarily affects our logic, images go deeper to connect with our feelings. A good picture can even create and cultivate new longings and desires. This is why marketers use photography so liberally.

There is another reason that images are so powerful in advertisements. Since text appeals to our logic, it can be challenged and debated. But how can you refute, or even carefully weigh, a message received through emotion? Consider the Marlboro story.

The Power of a Picture

In 1924 Philip Morris Tobacco launched the Marlboro brand as a cigarette for sophisticated women. When sales declined in the 1950s, they decided to do a 180-degree turn and market their product as a man's cigarette.[2] To accomplish this, they turned to the power of pictures. Many of us remember advertisements showing a tough cowboy on the Western range promoting the Marlboro brand. His rugged appearance, the spectacular wild landscape, and his determined facial expression spoke volumes. Here was a real man! Fearlessly pursuing his self-determined course, this man was unconcerned about weather, public opinion, ferocious animals, or anything else this wild world might throw at him. Looking out over his ranch, he was the epitome of self-confidence and self-reliance. In short, he was the brave, confident, rugged individual that many men long to be. The unspoken message? "Smoking Marlboro will make you like this man."

These advertisements were extremely successful. Thousands of men looked at those pictures, and the message connected with their inner longing. This was the kind of man they wanted to be! Countless men were motivated to purchase Marlboro due to this advertising blitz.

What if the Philip Morris company had used print instead of

pictures? Imagine a Marlboro advertisement using only text. "If you smoke Marlboro, you will become a strong, fearless, and courageous man. You won't fear the future or what other people think of you. Smoking our cigarettes will make you brave, valiant, and daring!"

This would be ineffective for obvious reasons. Everyone knows that smoking a particular brand of cigarette isn't going to change a man's character. But when good pictures are used, emotion and deep desire can overrun logic, causing us to make illogical choices. This is, of course, exactly what marketers want. Now take this further. If a still image is worth a thousand words, imagine the value and impact of moving imagery combined with sound!

Combining Sight and Sound

July 1, 1941. The Brooklyn Dodgers were preparing to play the Philadelphia Phillies in New York. The public was just starting to enjoy the miracle of watching baseball on their televisions. Just before the first pitch a short advertisement was aired. It was only ten seconds long with very little action, but that first television commercial changed the course of marketing.[3] At the time, advertisement agencies saw very little potential in TV. Radio was the dominant force in broadcasting, and one reputable advertising company had even asserted, "Evidence is mounting that TV will gain little headway for the duration." However, marketers soon began to grasp the potential in video. That first television commercial cost the Bulova watch company about four dollars to produce and was only seen by a few thousand people in New York.

Today, a single ad spot can cost millions of dollars to produce and broadcast. Even more incredible is how little they need to tell you about their products to be effective. Chanel, the French perfume company, paid $33 million for a television commercial in 2004. The advertisement was extremely successful, and Chanel's sales for the year rose to an all-time high. The short video featured a well-known actress and a writer who fall in love in the back seat of a taxi. Nothing in the video informs the potential purchaser about how the perfume is made, why it is better, or what costly ingredients it contains. It just tells a romantic short story and suggests that Chanel is involved.

In 2011 Chrysler Company paid $12 million to advertise their new Model 200 during the Super Bowl. The commercial was two minutes long, yet anyone wanting facts about the vehicle would have been disappointed. Nothing was mentioned about the engine, drivetrain, warranty, or comfortable interior. The entire commercial focused on a famous rapper driving his shiny black Chrysler in his hometown of Detroit.[4]

Why would a company spend millions of dollars for a commercial containing no facts about its product? Because the primary goal is not to connect with your logic, but with your emotions. A well-crafted video can transfer emotional content much faster than your mind can critique it. That is why videos are so useful to advertising agencies.

> A well-crafted video can transfer emotional content much faster than your mind can critique it.

But sight and sound are doing more than causing us to purchase unneeded products. They are also shaping our views and values.

CHAPTER FIFTEEN

ENTERTAINMENT— CHANGING OUR VIEWS AND VALUES

One of the first to grasp the incredible potential of electronic media to shape a culture's views and values was Adolf Hitler. Immediately following his dramatic rise to power in 1933, his Nazi Party took control of the Ministry of Public Enlightenment and Propaganda and flooded the airwaves with pro-Nazi information. Radio broadcasts transmitted a continual diet of Aryan idealism and national pride, interspersed with the best popular orchestra music available. Hitler knew the programing had to be entertaining to be accepted. To ensure that this message was heard, Hitler ordered the production of inexpensive radio sets and distributed them across Germany. These one-channel radios, known as the "People's Receivers," became the public's primary source of information. Speaker systems were set up in train stations, city centers, and anywhere else the public gathered. The German people, whether at home or in the market, were constantly surrounded by Nazi messages.

As television and the cinema became common in the 1930s, the Nazis immediately grasped the ability of this new media to shape public opinion. Between 1933 and 1945 the Nazi regime produced

1,090 films for the German public.[1] Life was difficult in Germany at the time, and families found the cinema a distraction from the grind of daily life. What many of them didn't realize was that these films were not being produced simply for their pleasure. They were deliberately designed to change the German people's views and values.

Some of these films were intended to develop a fear of surrounding countries. Movies featured valiant German martyrs being killed by evil and unjust communists. Others showed Germans outwitting unscrupulous and sneaky British spies. Many had a theme of Aryan superiority running throughout the script. Moviegoers couldn't help but leave feeling proud and hopeful about their nation and people, but also a little angry that their superiority wasn't recognized around the world. Films like *The Eternal Jew* were blatant anti-Semitic brainwashing. Presented as a documentary, this film depicted Jewish people as uncivilized and parasitic. Viewers couldn't help feeling angry that these people were being allowed to do so much damage.

Perhaps most impactful on the German people was how these films portrayed Hitler himself. He was presented not only as a powerful leader giving solutions for economic problems and delivering masterful orations before admiring throngs, but also as a caring father figure. Even while he was plotting cruel ways to torture innocent victims, films showed him comforting the sick in hospitals, affectionately playing with pets, and tenderly interacting with small children.

This propaganda was extremely effective. After the war commenced and negative news occasionally trickled back into Germany about inhumane tactics or innocent people being slaughtered, the public was skeptical. After all, with a loving man like Hitler in charge, the situation couldn't be too far out of line.

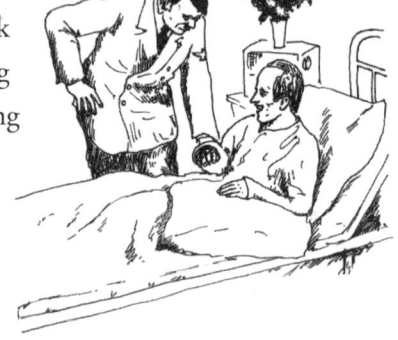

Media had conditioned them to approve of whatever he condoned.

We look back on that time in history and are perplexed. Couldn't the German people understand what was happening? Didn't a constant diet of slanted media raise any concerns? Incredibly, few were aware of how their views and values were being shaped because it was accomplished through entertainment. They laughed together at the comedies, cried together through emotional scenes, and rejoiced together when German heroes conquered. These movies were the talk on the street the next day. They couldn't wait for the next new film. But unknown to the public, they were allowing media to change their views, their values, and the very core of who they were.

Are we doing the same?

Receiving the Message

In his book *Media Effects*, author James Potter explains four ways in which we experience media. He calls them "exposure states," the first of which is the Attentional State. In this state you may not be concentrating on the message being received, but you are very aware of it. This might occur when you are clicking through websites or analyzing an advertisement. You are receiving information and assessing it in a fully aware state.

The second he calls the Automatic State. In this state you are receiving information but are not conscious this is occurring. Maybe you are reading a book while music is playing in the background. You are focused on the book and not keenly conscious of the music, yet it is being recorded subconsciously. This may or may not have much of an impact on your thoughts.

The third he calls the Transported State, where you are totally caught up in the message so that you lose track of time and place. This is the goal of the entertainment industry, and we will address this later.

The fourth is the Self-Reflexive State, where you are very aware of the message and your own processing of it. This might be during a poorly done television advertisement. You are aware of what they are trying to do, and you are not affected by it.

Let's return to the Transported State, since this is where our views and values are directly assaulted. In Potter's own words, this is where "people are swept away and 'enter' the message." He goes on to say that people in this state "lose track of their social worlds."[2]

The Transported State

The goal of every good movie director is to pull the viewer into this transported state. When a movie is well done, the viewer is drawn into the plot and feels the emotions, joy, and pain of the performer on the screen. The viewer becomes one with the actor. We understand why he feels the way he does, why he responds how he does, and we are there with him as each act unfolds. When the actor is sad, we are too, and when he rejoices, our spirits lift. The actor's passions and desires become ours and we, for the moment, disconnect from our own moral groundings and live vicariously through the actor. A movie director's ability to consistently draw viewers into this transported state determines his success and standing within the film industry. This is one of the factors that makes a "good" movie.

When a viewer allows himself to be drawn into the life of the actor, his own life is temporarily placed on hold. For many, this is an escape from painful reality; for others it is simply a way to pass the time. But we must understand this is not a neutral state. We are choosing, for the moment, to place ourselves into the hands of the movie director. We see life as the actor sees it. His concerns, fears, passions, and hopes become ours. For a time we are allowing the movie director to subtly steer our minds into loving what the actor loves, hating his enemies, and even joining the actor in illicit or immoral relationships. We assume we can temporarily hand our emotions, but not our morals, over to the director of the movie and pick up daily life as normal after it is over.

But is that possible? Can we, through the actor, participate in ungodly activities and come out unscathed? The answer is no, because the things we engage in have an impact on the inner core of who we are becoming.

C.S. Lewis wrote, "When you are behaving as if you loved someone, you will presently come to love him. If you injure someone you dislike, you will find yourself disliking him more."[3] Just like the inner part of us affects what we do outwardly, our outward activities also affect how we think and who we are becoming internally. The connection between the inner and the outer goes both ways. Jesus said, "If any man will do his will, he shall know of the doctrine, whether it be of God, or whether I speak of myself."[a] As we are obedient to the words of Jesus, something inside us changes, and we know in a fresh way who Jesus is.

> What reaches our eyes affects our minds and ultimately who we are.

I find it fascinating and sobering that even our ungodly secular society knows that what we watch has a powerful effect on what we become. This is why God told the children of Israel to write His law "upon the door posts of thine house, and upon thy gates."[b] I have never yet met an individual, regardless of his religious philosophy, who believes that allowing small children to watch horror movies is a good idea. What reaches our eyes affects our minds and ultimately who we are. Jesus made this connection when He said, "Whosoever looketh on a woman to lust after her hath committed adultery with her already in his heart."[c] These are sobering words, and they bring some unavoidable questions to our culture.

How many viewers, under the guise of entertainment, are entering this transported state and lusting vicariously through an actor on the screen? And even more seriously, how many professing followers of Jesus, believers who stand on the Word of God and openly proclaim their opposition to any shade of immorality, sit down in

---

[a] John 7:17
[b] Deuteronomy 11:20
[c] Matthew 5:28

front of a screen and enjoy living out an illicit relationship through a "good movie?" How does God see this, and what impact will this have on the church over time? Can a man continue to "take fire into his bosom"[d] and not be changed? Can a church?

Choosing to repeatedly be entertained by Hollywood will affect you. Initially, it will affect your feelings and emotions. Like the Germans in the 1930s, you will find yourself laughing, crying, and living exciting events through the media. Over time, entertainment will shape your views and values. You will find "normal" gradually changing, and you won't understand why. Hairstyles, clothes, and fashions you once viewed as appalling will seem acceptable, even attractive. You may even find yourself admiring people whose lives would at one time have been repulsive.

If you keep pursuing fulfillment in the decadent entertainment of our culture, something even more subtle and serious will occur. Your morals, the bedrock of who you are, will eventually change too. This should cause serious followers of Jesus Christ to carefully examine what they choose to watch.

---

[d] Proverbs 6:27

CHAPTER SIXTEEN

POP CULTURE VERSUS KINGDOM CULTURE

Pop culture, according to the dictionary, is "modern popular culture transmitted via the mass media and aimed particularly at younger people."[1] Pop culture has been around for many years, but due to the influx of technology, it is having a revolutionary influence on society. There was a time when people were driven by an underlying ideological belief. It may have been national pride, religion, or a foundational sense of right and wrong absorbed from a previous generation. Popular culture is different. It has no fixed political or religious ideology, but rather caters to what the masses of people want. As a result, pop culture has become synonymous with amusement. Entertainment is not only what we want, it has also become what we worship. Musicians, movie stars, and sports figures have become the leaders of pop culture. Entertainment is no longer a brief reprieve from normal activity. It has become a constant companion, the way people think, and America's leading religion all wrapped into one. Some of today's thinkers are promoting this shift, and Alexandre Philippe is one of these pop culture promoters.

Alexandre is a Swiss film director, and for him the logic is simple.

Politics, religion, social issues, cultural beliefs—all these value systems divide us. They inevitably create conflict and stress. But pop culture is something everyone can agree on. Good movies, football games, funny videos—these are the essence of pop culture, and Alexandre believes this is the content we should be promoting. He says this:

> Pop culture is a universal language. It manages in all of its seemingly trivial glory to make us dream and smile. To connect us across racial, political and social divides. It says something about us, about our better nature. So isn't it time for us to respect it, cherish it, and learn to preserve it? I say this with great urgency. The one thing that makes America so great to the rest of the world, above all else, is the fact that we are the first civilization in human history to have made fun important. And we must never, ever, ever, lose that![2]

Most do not take pop culture as seriously as Alexandre Philippe. Any thinking person is probably a little jarred by his comments. Should Americans be proud if their greatest contribution to the world is that we "have made fun important"? Would any sane individual argue that ignoring a problem by amusing ourselves is a viable solution? Yet the important question isn't what others think of pop culture. The real issue is this: Are you and your congregation aware of the impact pop culture is having, and how are you responding?

Harry Argo was born into a military family in 1956. His family had a tradition of serving in the armed forces, and after graduating from West Point, he focused on studying information technology, eventually graduating with a PhD. Harry professed belief in Christ in his twenties and was active in Protestant youth ministry. But as he continued to read the Bible and observe the lives of fellow believers, some issues began to trouble him.

Harry saw youth being destroyed by pop culture and technology.

These perils were damaging their real relationships and face-to-face communication. His studies had convinced him that the church was taking this topic too lightly, but he wasn't sure what to do. Then he heard about the Anabaptists—and went on a search. Were there really groups of people out there whose minds had not been saturated and damaged by electronic media? People who were not following pop culture?

Harry's first introduction to Anabaptist communities came in 2011. He was excited with what he found. Here were people who were not immersed in electronic technology or being led by pop culture. He embraced their beliefs and eventually joined an Anabaptist church. He continued studying technology and the sway of pop culture. As churches learned about his knowledge of this topic, they invited him to give lectures. As Harry interacted with Anabaptist churches, he noticed that while some were doing well, others were struggling.

Unconcerned About Others

Some of the church groups Harry visited tend to withdraw from society and shun technology. They are fearful of pop culture and have little interest in evangelizing beyond their own people. While Harry appreciated some things about this segment, he believed they could learn something from a man named Carl Von Clausewitz.

Carl Von Clausewitz was a Prussian general who was involved in numerous military campaigns in the early 1800s. He was also a prolific writer, and two hundred years later his theories and fighting tactics are still used in military schools. While in West Point, Harry Argo was exposed to Clausewitz's teachings, and one of the lessons they received was this: "Defense is the strongest form of combat in which you always lose."

An army that focuses exclusively on defense and preservation, regardless of how strong they are, will ultimately lose the battle. The enemy will continue to attack from every angle until eventually the defense is penetrated. Successful armies, on the other hand, not only have a strong defense, but also an offensive goal and strategy.

Churches are the same way. Focusing only on strong defense can provide false security. It is easy to believe we are strong because we have poured great amounts of energy into defense. But God didn't intend for His church to just hunker down and preserve what it has been given. To have God's blessing, churches also need to have their eye on accomplishing His goals, reaching out to others, and taking ground back from the enemy.

> God didn't intend for His church to just hunker down and preserve what it has been given.

Unconcerned About Pop Culture

There was another group of Anabaptist churches that alarmed Harry Argo. This segment seemed unconcerned about pop culture and was failing to take meaningful defensive measures against it. When Harry attended evangelical churches that ignored Jesus' teaching on divorce and remarriage, mentioning the topic immediately caused tension. "The leaders simply had too much to lose," Harry told me, "and they knew they would lose members if they addressed the Biblical teaching on divorce and remarriage."

Harry is finding a similar apprehension in some Anabaptist church leaders when he broaches the topic of pop culture and how their youth are using technology. Watching occasional movies, keeping up on sports, using social media, and viewing funny videos have become a way of life. Leaders know their people would resist if they were asked to give up electronic entertainment. "It's like they haven't come to grips with the fact that you can't mix pop culture with kingdom culture," Harry said.

Cultural Alarm

Once again there seems to be more concern about pop culture in *secular* society than in Christian circles. In recent years secular scholars and patriotic Americans have been voicing concern.

What happens when citizens are more concerned with following the daily lives of celebrities than they are about war, famine, or the national budget? How can a country like this continue? As Neil Postman has queried, "How is it that we've fought three wars that no one really seems to care about, allowed mortgage scams and national debt to crater our economy, and squandered an immense human capital lead on the rest of the world?"

It's a rhetorical question. Shouldn't someone be alarmed? Postman continues, trying to put his finger on what has changed.

> As a nation, we've always loved fantasy, from science fiction books to Hollywood celebrities. Television, radio, and print have been filled with mindless drivel from day one as a way to ease our troubled minds. The switch isn't our need to escape from the harsh realities of the world, but that the escape has become the way we actually define the reality. We are no longer escaping from the world into pop culture, we are living it twenty-four hours a day without really caring about the truth. We've entered a deep sleep and resent anyone who tries to wake us from our slumber with the downer of facts, figures, and true life.[3]

Loyal citizens of a democratic country have every right to be alarmed when its voters have more interest in entertainment than reality. It is only right to ask how long a country like this can even exist as a nation. But what about the church? Shouldn't those who are trying to follow Jesus be even more concerned? A love of pop culture is irreconcilable with the kingdom of God, and trying to merge them will inevitably create conflict.

Cultural Incompatibility

Pop culture exists to bring pleasure. Consuming digital entertainment is successful if you are amused and entertained. Did you like the movie? Was the video funny? Pop culture places *self* squarely on the throne, and your pleasure and satisfaction are of primary concern.

The kingdom of God exists to bring glory to God. The Gospel of Jesus Christ is successful when sinful men repent, change, and begin living to please God. Are the changes in my life bringing glory to God? Are my actions blessing others and demonstrating Jesus? Kingdom culture puts God on the throne, and His pleasure and glory are paramount.

Despite their incompatibility, churches feel pressured to marry these two, and the reason is simple. When churchgoers consume pop culture throughout the week, it isn't easy to make the switch on Sunday. Electronic entertainment is designed to be about *you*. Being asked on Sundays to relinquish the throne we have grown to love through the week isn't easy. If the modern church is to keep attendance up, some concessions must be made.

Somehow we miss the hypocrisy. You cannot accurately present a self-denying Gospel that focuses on God through self-focused entertainment. That's like putting up a billboard message that says radio is a better marketing tool than billboards. The medium is diametrically opposed to the message. When churches go down this road, the Gospel message becomes distorted.

Interestingly enough, non-Christians like Neil Postman see this incongruity better than the majority of modern Christians. He writes: "Christianity is a demanding and serious religion. When it is delivered as easy and amusing, it is another kind of religion altogether." Postman was raised in a nonobservant Jewish home, and he writes from a Judeo-Christian perspective. His writings are powerful and have been widely used by Christian teachers, even though he apparently made no religious profession.[4]

God does not intend that we live drab or humorless lives. He wants us to enjoy rich relationships and heartfelt laughter. He created us to enjoy our world and each other. I don't believe Jesus received invitations to dine with publicans and sinners[a] due to His refusal to smile or hear a humorous story. But when unbelievers are concerned about popular culture, sociologists are alarmed about the impact of constant electronic entertainment, and scholars are worried about the future of our nation, shouldn't the church be taking notice?

What's Wrong with It?

Have we really assumed we can constantly amuse ourselves through mass media, perpetual news feeds, sports updates, and other ever-changing venues of electronic entertainment and come out unscathed? Entertainment is addictive—it feeds inner cravings that grow if nourished. When we ask what is wrong with this video,

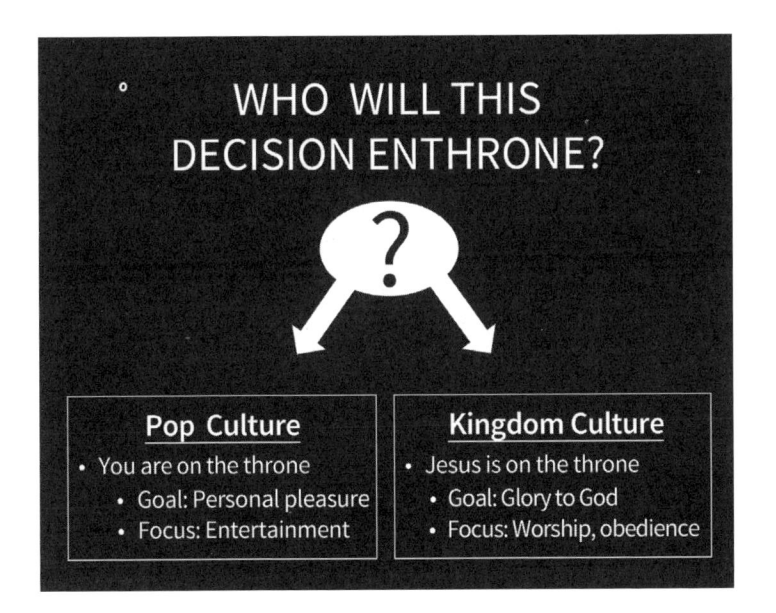

> **WHO WILL THIS DECISION ENTHRONE?**
>
> | Pop Culture | Kingdom Culture |
> |---|---|
> | • You are on the throne | • Jesus is on the throne |
> | • Goal: Personal pleasure | • Goal: Glory to God |
> | • Focus: Entertainment | • Focus: Worship, obedience |

movie, or electronic entertainment, we are asking the wrong question. The real question is, "Who does this enthrone?" Author Gary Gilley strikes at the crux of our dilemma. "The problem is that the main business of entertainment is to please the crowd, but the main purpose of authentic Christianity is to please the Lord."[5] If we are

---

[a] Matthew 11:18, 19; Luke 7:34

going to survive this narcissistic culture and its preoccupation with entertainment, we need to understand that pop culture and authentic Christianity cannot coexist.

Christianity, from its inception, has always required difficult choices and total allegiance. God will not share His throne. For example, when addressing wealth, Jesus made this profound statement: "No man can serve two masters: for either he will hate the one, and love the other; or else he will hold to the one, and despise the other. Ye cannot serve God and mammon."[b] Though Jesus was emphatic that serving money and serving God are mutually exclusive paths, Christians have tried to do both ever since.

We are having a similar difficulty with pop culture. It feels so good and seems so right to our flesh that we would love to find a path of accommodation, and it is difficult to walk away from electronic entertainment once we have become accustomed to it. Why is this? Pop culture and Christianity are obviously on incompatible trajectories. So why do we have such difficulty letting it go?

---

[b] Matthew 6:24

CHAPTER SEVENTEEN

"BEING BORED IS BORING!"

Recently I saw a sign that stated a recurring theme of our day: "Bored of being bored, because being bored is boring!" Everyone, it seems, is on a quest to avoid boredom. Monotony is out; excitement is in. Constant interaction and entertainment are expected.

A few years ago I boarded an overseas flight, and the entertainment system on the plane was experiencing difficulty. The flight attendants made a lengthy announcement apologizing for the fact that there would be no video available during the flight. They even passed out little cards expressing regret at this unfortunate turn of events. Despite their efforts, many passengers were not appeased. There was muttering all around and the popular consensus was, "It isn't right for them to expect us to sit here for hours with nothing to look at!" After all, we might get bored!

It hasn't always been this way.

On August 21, 1858, the first of seven debates took place between Abraham Lincoln and Stephen Douglas. Douglas started by speaking for one hour, and Lincoln then had an hour and a half to reply. When Lincoln concluded, Douglas was given a half hour to counter Lincoln's rebuttal. Imagine a crowd hanging around for three hours to listen to two politicians. Remarkably, this debate was much shorter than these two men were used to. A few years earlier, these same men had debated in Peoria, Illinois. Douglas began by talking for three hours. When it was time for Lincoln's rebuttal, he noted that it was five o'clock in the evening and his response would take as long as Douglas's. He suggested that everyone go home and then return for another four hours of talk, which is what they did.[1]

What makes this more startling is that these men were not even running for office at the time. They were debating the issue of slavery, and people were interested enough to listen to seven hours of oratory on the topic. Contrast this to the 2016 United States presidential debates, where the moderator asked a question and each candidate was given just two minutes to respond.[2] Just long enough for a couple of choice statements for the next day's news and a few gaffes for talk show hosts and late-night comedians to rehash. In today's culture, winners aren't determined by facts or well-considered positions. A zippy one-liner trumps good content and is the best way to ensure your name is in the headlines.

This is not to say that people in the mid-1800s were more intellectual or even had a better grasp of the issues of the day. Much of those long speeches was worthless hyperbole, a source of entertainment, an opportunity for the orator to display his oratory skills. Politicians then, like today, used debates as an opportunity to garner support. That part hasn't changed. But what about the crowd? How many people today would stick around for seven hours to listen to a couple of men pontificate on a topic? We still like information, but we want it quick, succinct, and preferably with pictures. We have become a sound-bite culture, and I suspect most of the crowd would leave long before a seven-hour debate was complete. Today we want news delivered in a way that is brief, engaging, entertaining, and certainly never boring.

Historically, boredom was primarily a problem among the rich.[3][a]

---

[a] The word *boredom* wasn't even a word until 1852 when Charles Dickens published his book *Bleak House*.

They were the only ones with the luxury of sitting and wishing for something to occupy their time. While the poor were scrambling to survive, the wealthy lived tedious, monotonous lives. As one writer has noted: "It is surely not coincidental that all the earliest citations of the word *bore* in the Oxford English Dictionary—from the mid-eighteenth century—come from the correspondence of aristocrats and nobility."[4]

For most people in the Dark Ages, life was short, difficult, and often miserable.[b] They didn't hear in church that life was supposed to be happy. Rather, Christians were taught that inner joy amid difficulty was possible.

Today both secular and Christian culture insinuate that we should be in a constant state of happiness. Happy is the expected norm, and its absence is cause for concern. We are surrounded by machines designed to accomplish our difficult daily tasks, and we have extra time to pursue pleasure, but for some reason, boredom is the result instead. And increasingly, people are turning to electronic technology for relief.

Cure or Cause?
Is electronic technology the solution to boredom? Everyone seems to be tethered to an electronic device. Even when engaged in a business meeting or a face-to-face conversation, our gadgets are within arm's reach. Like a parachute cord hanging at the ready, these devices promise protection anytime the frightful prospect of boredom rears its dreadful head. But are they an effective antidote?

Increasingly researchers are concerned that, far from *curing* boredom, this technology may be part of the cause. British psychologist Sandi Mann addressed this issue in an article titled "Why Are We So Bored?" She argues that constant access to entertainment is partly the cause:

---

[b] Philip Rieff, a Jewish sociologist, studied this shift in expectations. Even though he was not a Christian, Rieff understood that Jesus had never promised His followers constant happiness. "Formerly, if men were miserable, they went to church, so as to find the rationale of their misery; they did not expect to be happy—this idea is Greek, not Christian or Jewish." —Philip Rieff, *The Triumph of the Therapeutic*, The University of Chicago, Chicago, Illinois, 1966, p. 38.

The more entertained we are the more entertainment we need in order to feel satisfied. The more we fill our world with fast-moving, high-intensity, ever-changing stimulation, the more we get used to that and the less tolerant we become of lower levels.[5]

Many of us have experienced this. After exposure to fast-paced entertainment, we find that slower-paced activities, such as interacting with family or reading our Bible are boring. When you flood your mind with constant stimulation, something within subtly shifts. Instead of reducing monotony, you are training your mind to expect more than the average day can supply, and boredom increases. Normal activities, events that at one time brought you great pleasure, now seem mundane, ordinary, and dull.

I have heard people complain that their family Christmas gatherings are no longer very enjoyable. At one time, they planned for the coming event, talked about it, and couldn't wait to get together to play games and interact with people they hadn't seen since the last Christmas. Now they gather and eat a meal, but as soon as the conversation lags, out come the devices, and human interaction stops. Even the family Christmas can't compete with the fast-paced electronic stimulation available on our screens. Technology is teaching us to expect endless excitement and action—more than real life can deliver. This is having a powerful effect on young children who are constantly exposed to a media-saturated culture.

> Technology is teaching us to expect endless excitement and action—more than real life can deliver.

Hidden Threat to the Home

Most discussions I hear regarding the dangers of electronic media revolve around content. How will certain movies or violent games affect our children? Another threat that is harder to quantify, but may be just as deadly, is technology's ability to make human interactions and relationships seem uninteresting. Our children may find real people tedious and choose to retreat to their devices to escape interaction with these "boring" people. In his book *The Tech-Wise Family*, Andy Crouch makes a profound observation. "The more you entertain children, the more bored they will get."⁶ He isn't saying we shouldn't play with our children. But we must not ignore an important truth. Some of the happiest children I have ever seen live in developing countries and have never visited a toy store. They make cars out of pop bottles, create dolls from rags, and develop games that require only sticks and rocks. They have never experienced toys that beep, talk, or sing and are unaware that batteries are required to have fun. Little effort has been expended helping them avoid boredom, and consequently, little is required to keep them entertained.

On the other end of the spectrum are children who have grown up expecting constant stimuli. I remember working in a very wealthy home. The "playroom" was the size of a small toy store, and there were literally aisles of toys available for just one little boy's pleasure. Yet I think I can safely say he was the most bored child I have ever met. He had been trained to expect constant pleasure in life, and his world was letting him down.

Leaders in the electronic technology industry seem more concerned about its effect on their children than anyone. In 2007 Bill Gates, then CEO of Microsoft, noticed that his daughter was developing an unhealthy attachment to a video game. Consequently, he implemented a cap on screen time, and Gates didn't allow his children to have their own cell phones until they were fourteen years old, a late age for many in the secular world.⁷

In a 2010 interview with the *New York Times*, Steve Jobs, founder of Apple Computer and public promoter of its products, was asked how his children were enjoying Apple's new iPad. "They haven't used it," Jobs replied. "We limit how much technology our kids use at home."⁸

Sean Parker, founding president of Facebook, confessed in a 2017 interview, "It probably interferes with productivity in weird ways. God only knows what it's doing to our children's brains."[9]

Are these men seeing things some of us are missing?

Some children have lost their curiosity, their desire to be with people, and even the ability to relate to other humans. Their only emotion when separated from their device is perpetual boredom. I have also met the opposite. I can think of parents who have purposely restricted their children's use of technology. They promote games and learning activities which rely heavily on reading and human interaction. Their children are naturally inquisitive and enthusiastic to learn. They thrive on human interaction and can't wait to meet new people. These are children who see life and nature as a pathway of discovery. While technology isn't the entire reason for the difference, there is a connection. It is difficult, if not impossible, for daily life to be as interesting and engaging as the material available through electronic media.

Threat to Our Church Communities

Two more threats need to be addressed. First, electronic technology can damage our ability to communicate face to face, and I don't believe we fully understand the ramifications. Face-to-face relationships demand patience. Life moves too fast, and we are often too busy to sit, listen, ponder, and learn from others. When we lose this aptitude, we are also losing our ability to maintain healthy church communities. Face-to-face communication is a building block of community. If we are going to have strong churches in a media-saturated culture, we need to give careful attention to this.

The second threat is that we can become more enthralled with technology than the magnificence of God's creation. Some of the gadgets being produced today are nothing short of amazing. The ability to compute rapidly, store massive amounts of data, or video conference with multiple people around the globe is incredible.

Almost every week we hear of some breakthrough, a new development or timesaving device on the market. Consequently, we can't help but think, talk, and marvel about the wonderful technological advances taking place in our world.

Is this subtly taking the place of our worship of God? Are we still enthralled by a brilliant sunrise? Or are we more dazzled by the technology that informs us exactly when it will occur? Do we still take time to look up at the incredible night sky? Or are we more astonished at the gadgets that tell us, with astounding precision, the names of the constellations we are viewing? I believe technology can be used to glorify the Creator. But if God is to remain preeminent, it will take conscious effort to keep our focus on Him and be amazed at His power, not at the technology that is simply revealing His majesty.

The Real Question

While electronic communication can hinder relationships, it also has the power to help us communicate more effectively, share our struggles, and reach out to the hurting and lost. It can distract us from the wonderful creation that surrounds us, but it can also increase our awe of God as we learn more about the complexities of creation. The question isn't whether technology is good or bad. Rather, we should ask if it is helping us draw closer to God and others. The reality is, most of us living in the developed world are bored much more easily than we once were. It is time we look closely, both personally and as church communities, at the impact this is having on our walk with God.

CHAPTER EIGHTEEN

CIRCUMVENTING GOD'S DESIGN

It should be clear to any student of the New Testament that God intends for His church to demonstrate His character and deliver His message to a lost world. This is evident in Jesus' prayer just before going to the cross. He prayed that His disciples would care for each other and become one in Him. Yet this desire for unity had a greater purpose.

> That they all may be one; as thou, Father, art in me, and I in thee, that they also may be one in us: *that the world may believe that thou hast sent me.* ²²And the glory which thou gavest me I have given them; that they may be one, even as we are one: ²³I in them, and thou in me, that they may be made perfect in one; *and that the world may know that thou hast sent me,* and hast loved them, as thou hast loved me."[a] (emphasis added)

Jesus intended for His church to love in such a way that others

---

[a] John 17:21–23

would notice. We have some basic human needs and inner longings, and God has provided the church as a place where these longings can be fulfilled. But when God offers a solution, Satan quickly proposes a counterfeit.

Living in close community and loving each other sacrificially is hard, and all of us are tempted to gravitate toward alternatives. Circumventing God's design didn't start with electronic technology, but it has made it much easier. In this chapter I would like to look at some basic needs we all have, how God intends that we fulfill these needs, and some ways Satan is using technology to bypass God's design.

Need to Belong

This inner longing is unmistakable, whether in a child on the playground wanting to be included, a teenager afraid she isn't part of the "in" group, or those who are older and still wondering how they fit in. We have a deep need to belong to something bigger, and God has designed the church family to fulfill this need. Whether you are single or married, young or old, rich or poor, the church should be a place where everyone feels included.

Recently I was talking with a young man, and when I asked about his social life he quickly responded, "Oh, I have over two hundred friends on Facebook!" In other words, don't worry about me, I am attached to a large community and have loads of friends—I belong! He was taking consolation in virtual community.

Close community requires sacrifice. Consequently, people are increasingly avoiding it. They find connecting electronically so much easier. Technology enables people to build communities with those they agree with, rather than working out conflicts with those they live

> Technology enables people to build communities with those they agree with, rather than working out conflicts with those they live with.

with. Circumventing the hard work of building authentic communities also keeps us from learning more about ourselves. This is why virtual community is so tempting.

Shane Hipps describes the shallowness of virtual community like this: "It provides just enough connection to keep us from pursuing real intimacy. . . . In a virtual community, our contacts involve very little real risk and demand even less of us personally. Vulnerability is optional. . . . Virtual community is infinitely more virtual than it is communal. It's a bit like cotton candy: it goes down easy and satiates our immediate hunger, but it doesn't provide much in the way of sustainable nutrition. Not only that, but our appetite is spoiled. We no longer feel the need to participate in authentic community."[1]

After a recent backlash against Facebook, I read an article by a Christian commentator titled *How Social Media Has Become a Sad Substitute for True Community*. She observed the mass exodus from this network and read the comments from disgruntled users, trying to discern why they were switching.

> It appears as if people are looking for a specific sort of service—an online hangout spot that's both "nice" and "real." They want a platform where they can share their true selves without fear of judgment and without starting arguments. In a way, what they really want is community—a group of people with whom they can share their struggles and receive support without also receiving condemnation. In my mind, the type of community they're looking for sounds a lot like what God intended for the Church to be. As one body with many members, the Church is a place for Christ-followers to come together in unity, flourishing in love and generosity toward one another and toward those outside of the Church.[2]

Something within each of us longs for the blessing of true

community. But do we understand what is lost when we neglect God's best? The goal of authentic, self-denying communities isn't just to fulfill our inner needs. It is also to demonstrate God's principles to a lost world. When we neglect close community and attempt to replace it with social media to satisfy our need to belong, we are settling for Satan's substitute. His offerings are always less than God's best.

Care in Old Age

All of us are getting older, and someday may no longer be able to care for ourselves. Once again, God has a plan to meet this need. He has placed us in biological families and given us instructions. Paul addresses this in his letter to Timothy, reminding him that it is the family's responsibility to care for those who can no longer take care of themselves. If the family isn't able, then the church community is to fill in and assist as needed.[b] This is God's intent, and many of us have seen the beauty of this plan in action. Of course, this isn't always convenient. It often requires children and church communities to change their plans and priorities. So once again, substitute programs are available.

During the past few decades, many older people have been placed in rest homes, but even this is getting harder. Not only is this expensive, but in some countries it is increasingly difficult to find qualified, willing staff. Consider Japan. With a declining birth rate and more than one quarter of its population now over sixty-five years old,[3] Japan has a major problem. Who will care for their elderly? By 2065 they are projecting that 40 percent of their population will be over sixty-five. Japan's younger generation is hardworking and still trying to get ahead financially. Who is going to be willing to stay home to help their aging parents? One option is relying on foreign workers. But nationalistic pride has made this solution difficult, so once again people are turning to technology.

Today in Japan you will find many rest homes using robots to

---

[b] 1 Timothy 5:3–16

care for their elderly. The robots speak with human voices, provide companionship, bring food and drinks, remind the forgetful to take their medicine, and are even capable of lifting patients out of bed and into their wheelchairs.[4] These machines never complain, get tired, go on strike, or ask for time off. As one proponent of this movement has said, "People are risky; robots are safe."[5] Japan isn't alone, and as birth rates in developed counties continue to decline, other countries are sure to follow. But is this really progress or an improvement on God's original design?

As a young teenager, I watched my parents bring my grandmother into our home. She suffered from dementia, and I am sure if she were still alive, machines could care for her physical needs. In fact, she might not even have known the difference. But what about those looking on? Watching my parents put their plans on hold made a profound impression on my life. I knew they were giving up travel and activities they would have enjoyed. And what about our neighbors and our community? Families and churches who lovingly care for their elderly are demonstrating the character of God to a world searching for meaning. Losing this means losing an integral part of Christ's vision for His church. Let's look at other ways that technology threatens to undermine God's design for His church.

The Need to Confess

James writes, "Confess your faults one to another, and pray one for another, that ye may be healed."[c] Many of us have seen and experienced the blessing of confession. We understand that one of the beauties of a healthy, vibrant church family is having a safe place to unload struggles. But when churches fail to provide this support, many turn to technology. Confessional websites have emerged where one can anonymously confess the sin that has been burdening him and try to find relief. Humans have an inner longing to acknowledge transgressions publicly, and these sites attempt to fill this need.

---

[c] James 5:16

Demand is so high that many high schools and colleges now have their own pages where students can anonymously pour out their failures, fears, and disappointments.

I have never visited one of these websites. I've been told that some of the confessions are so raw and descriptive that a good Internet filter won't allow you to visit. Those who have studied these sites are shocked at what they contain. There are confessions from married men who are living outwardly happy lives while involved in illicit relationships with other men in their church. Women who lament having aborted a child. Individuals who have abused others. Due to the demand, some churches have succumbed to this pressure and developed their own sites. Obviously, we have an inner need to confess sin. Yet is this really what God has in mind?

A pastor from one of these churches was interviewed, and after sharing how successful the site has been, he succinctly put his finger on its fatal flaw. Because the site is anonymous, there is nothing a pastor can do to help. "Knowing that so many people I see every week look so normal on the outside, and yet inside there is so much pain, that has been surprising. When you hear about it in their own words, it's hard to bear."[6] One can imagine the dilemma this pastor finds himself in. Imagine looking out over a large congregation each Sunday. You know that many in your congregation are struggling and hurting, yet due to the anonymous nature of the website, there is no way to know who needs help. Is this what God had in mind? Maybe we need to return to God's original design: close, committed church communities where individuals can not only confess, but also find someone to walk with them through the difficulty.

The Need to Conquer

God has given men a natural desire to overcome obstacles, solve problems, and conquer enemies. In our broken world there is no shortage of legitimate ways for a man to satisfy this need. Whether providing for his family, overcoming disease in the cornfield, repairing machinery, or becoming involved in some aspect of spiritual warfare, man has many opportunities to fulfill this need to overcome and conquer. Once again, men have found a way to bypass God's design and feed this inner craving through technology—electronic gaming.

When simple computer games first were introduced in the 1950s, no one could have anticipated the coming phenomena. Play a few rounds of tic-tac-toe, and most people were ready to move on. Even in the 1970s and early 1980s, games were very basic, yet interest was increasing. Computing power, stunning graphics, and remarkable audio capabilities continued to grow. Today's displays are so lifelike that people sit engrossed for hours. Electronic gaming has become so addictive that support groups have been formed and addiction treatment clinics set up to deal with this problem. The American Psychiatric Association even includes video gaming addiction as a mental health disorder.[7]

On electronic devices, many physically healthy young men are trying to fulfill their God-given desire to conquer. They fight enemies in online warfare, overcome wild beasts in a virtual jungle, or build and defend their castles and kingdoms vicariously through an online avatar. Research shows that this trend may even be affecting the labor market. Men are choosing to stay home from work to engage in online gaming.[8] However fun such games might be, what is the emotional cost to children whose father is more interested in winning a virtual game than interacting with them? This also brings a financial burden as the family is constrained by a reduced paycheck.

Perhaps a more pertinent question for the church is this: How does God regard His children frittering away their time in this type of worthless endeavor?

Some of these electronic diversions lead to immoral fantasy and have been extremely destructive to marriages. One trend is websites where individuals anonymously live exciting virtual lives. Users create their own identities, meet other virtual people also pretending to be someone they are not, develop relationships, get married, even purchase virtual property. People disillusioned with real life can escape for a time. Many users become involved in immoral online relationships, live out their explicit fantasies, distance themselves from reality, and try in vain to find fulfillment in something that doesn't even exist. Technology is not the root problem here. It is simply being used to deal with pain and disillusionment in life, a result of human depravity. Reading this calls to mind the description in Genesis of the state of man before the flood. "And God saw that the wickedness of man was great in the earth, and that every imagination of the thoughts of his heart was only evil continually."[d]

Assisting the Poor

There are other areas where men are looking to technological solutions instead of Christianity. Consider poverty alleviation. From its very beginning, the Christian church has been known for reaching out to the poor and downtrodden. It was a focus in the early church.[e] During an epidemic in the second century, the famous physician Galen got out of Rome as quickly as possible, while the Christians stayed to help the sick. The early church leader Cyprian almost welcomed the great epidemic of his time, because it was an opportunity for the church to give witness to the hope that was within them.[f] During the plagues of the Dark Ages, believers were the ones who stayed to help while others ran. Helping the poor has always been part of the church's mission. Yet many people promote technology as the best solution for global poverty today.[g] If everyone could access the Internet, we are told, everything would be wonderful.

Anywhere you go in the world, the cry is the same. "We need more technology!" In some ways, technology is a huge blessing in poor countries. It can improve healthcare, enhance education, and

---

[d] Genesis 6:5

[e] Acts 11:28–30; 2 Corinthians 8:14; Galatians 2:10

[f] "The best of the Greco-Roman scientists knew of no way to treat epidemics other than to avoid all contact with those who had the disease. And this they did, often evacuating entire towns, being afraid to visit one another." —Charles E. Moore, "Pandemic Love," <https://www.plough.com/en/topics/faith/discipleship/pandemic-love>, accessed on August 16, 2018.

[g] Recently I read an article titled, "Mobile Phones Are the Greatest Poverty-Reducing Tech Ever," with the subheading stating, *and possibly Africa's only real source of economic growth.*

allow farmers to find buyers and ways to transport crops to markets. Wireless technology has visibly improved their economy and living standard.

But the underlying cause of material poverty in our world isn't the lack of technology. As long as men have corrupt hearts and minds, poverty will exist. Yet increasingly, the church, Biblical teaching, and integrity are not seen as the solution to the world's problems—technology is. God intended that His church be known for helping the poor. Unfortunately, the church is rarely mentioned anymore in discussions regarding poverty alleviation. As one technology author argues, technology "contains more goodness than anything else we know."[9] What a shame that people are not saying this about the church! Perhaps our negligence as followers of Jesus in reaching out to the poor has allowed technology to fill this role.

Jesus wants His people to demonstrate His love and truth through loving, committed church communities. Instead, science and innovation, for many, has become the answer to the problems we face. To survive this tech tsunami, we need to actively seek God personally, support each other in loving close community, and have a clear vision of what God is calling His church to accomplish.

PART FOUR 4

WHERE ARE WE?

CHAPTER NINETEEN

THE CURRENT QUANDARY

London traffic had been a major problem for years, and in the 1830s a novel idea was proposed. Why not move the traffic to a railway beneath the large metropolis, with a tunnel under the Thames River itself? This idea was kicked around for years, but the costs were high and the public wasn't very excited about the prospect of traveling underground like moles. But eventually the idea caught on. Construction began, and in 1863 the Metropolitan Railway began transporting London commuters. Those first trains were primitive affairs, gas-lit wooden carriages pulled by steam locomotives. It would have required a bit of bravery to board one of those contraptions and descend into the bowels of the city. But in 1863 it was cutting-edge technology.

Through the years the system has improved and expanded, and today 1.37 billion passengers travel through these tunnels each year.[1] "The Tube," as it is affectionately known to the British, is a major part of English culture. With 270 stations, (some more than 150 feet below the surface) and 249 miles of track,[2] it is like a city under the city. The original planners back in the mid-1800s couldn't have imagined how many people would eventually travel through those tunnels they were digging. The entire project is an engineering marvel, but today it has one major problem. These tunnels are getting hot.

In 1900 the average tunnel temperature was around 57 degrees Fahrenheit. Today some routes are mobile saunas with high humidity and temperatures up to 95 degrees.[3] Businessmen leave their air-conditioned offices and arrive home drenched with sweat. Millions of people ponder the irony while fanning themselves and mopping their brows. Here they live in one of the most modern cities in the world, and they can't even get air conditioning on their subway.

So what is the problem? The original tunnels are too narrow to allow heat to escape. There was no way the original engineers could have envisioned millions of passengers, a constant flow of trains, and the immense amount of heat this would generate. An estimated half of this heat is a result of braking the trains. The tunnels are just large enough to let trains though, but not large enough to allow modern air conditioning units.

All manner of proposals have been presented, from the unusual to the absurd, such as putting blocks of ice in each car or drilling ventilation shafts down from the surface. While the debate continues, the British grumble and sweat it out. Originally, the tunnels were so cool they were advertised as a way to escape the summer heat on the surface. But times and conditions have changed. Today, the city continues to explore creative cooling options, and I am confident that the situation will eventually be resolved. But it will not be easy. The infrastructure that served them well in the past is a major frustration today.

As I watch conservative Anabaptist churches wrestle with this issue of technology, I see an interesting parallel. Church leaders who try to help their people maintain some level of separation from the world usually feel insecure about how they are handling electronic technology. Some take consolation in the fact that other groups are doing worse. But most are concerned. They sense that something vital is being lost and are not sure what to do. Perhaps most perplexing of all, governing methods that seemed to work so well in the past seem ineffective against this new threat.

Conservative Infrastructure

Following the Industrial Revolution, churches had to decide how much change to accept. Some were cautious, but the majority tended to assimilate into surrounding culture. After the turn of the century, the pace really picked up, and conservative churches began to develop an infrastructure to deal with this flood of choices. Automobiles, telephones, rapidly changing dress styles—all of these issues placed tremendous pressure on churches. How much should they accept? Looking back, it is apparent that churches that took a more cautious view of cultural change did better at maintaining some basic Biblical doctrines. Church leaders were discovering there was safety in just saying no.

During the 1930s and '40s, public radio broadcasts became popular, and churches had to decide what to do. Would bringing a radio into the home be a blessing or not? Churches debated the issue, and I remember my father talking about the tension it created. Most of the content was good at that time, and a family could sit and listen to gospel music right in their home. Some said if you didn't like what you were hearing, you could always turn it off. Yet there was a fear that this device might threaten family life, and for many churches the potential loss was greater than the perceived gain. Consequently, many conservative churches chose to say no to the radio. Looking back, most would say that this decision blessed them for the next fifty years. They had prayerfully considered this new technology, said no, and found that this took care of the issue.

In the 1950s it was television. Opinions differed, but this time it was a little easier. Conservative churches were seeing negative effects in churches that had not taken a stand against the radio, and they had learned something. Saying no to the inroads of technology was worthwhile and effective. So once again conservative churches stood against this new threat and said no. And again, that decision was clearly a wise move. No one could have predicted the amount of violence and immorality that television would someday deliver. For decades our churches and families have been blessed by the decision to say no. Men of God cautiously considered new technology and proved again that saying no is the best response.

And then came the Internet.

The Dilemma That Won't Disappear

When the Internet first appeared on the horizon, no one could have imagined the possibilities. Even some of the early developers saw little potential. For many church leaders, it looked like another electronic technology. They could address it with a simple "no" and move on to other things.

For some reason, this issue hasn't been as easy to solve.

As I have listened to many leaders from various constituencies talk about their church's difficulty in dealing with the Internet, they seem perplexed. Like the British businessmen sweating in London's subway, they don't understand why things must be this difficult. For many years their infrastructure worked so well. Why isn't the Internet as easy to deal with as radio and television were? Some fellowships have had this issue on the front burner for years. They gather periodically and try once again to resolve their differences, hoping for a creative solution that will allow them to maintain a safe position while keeping their constituency from further fragmentation. Yet year after year the debate rages on. As one Amish man recently told me, "Today's technology is pointing out a flaw in how we do church." The finely honed infrastructure that served so well for so long doesn't seem to be working. Something is different about this one. But how is it different?

Some church leaders, even after years of unsettledness, still believe the Internet is like radio and television, and churches just need to say no. It will be painful, they say, like it was for those who said no to other electronic innovations. But the long-term results will be worthwhile. Others disagree. Unlike radio or television, which are primarily vehicles for entertainment, the Internet is increasingly a necessary business tool. Without it, operating a business will be difficult at best.

Who is right? If the infrastructure that our ancestors developed isn't effective in dealing with this issue, what does work? Are there any churches out there that have discovered an effective approach to this problem?

How Are Conservative Anabaptists Doing?

To answer this question, I conducted a series of personal interviews within the larger conservative Anabaptist community. I wanted to discover the approaches various groups are taking and the results they are seeing. Are any groups effectively addressing this issue? Some say the church needs to retreat further from this decadent society, even if this means changing our occupations and way of life. Others disagree, arguing that the real issue is a spiritual one. If a man is born of God and being led by the Holy Spirit, he won't have trouble using the Internet and electronic technology. After all, your computer only delivers what you ask for. So who is right?

I began by creating two lists of questions. The first was specifically for church leaders and older members of church communities. I wanted to know their vision for their church, what approach they are taking with electronic technology, and how satisfied they are with the results. I also wanted to know how connected they are with their youth and whether they are comfortable communicating with or confronting them on this issue.

The second list of questions was for youth from the same congregations. How is electronic technology actually being used? What kind of impact is it having on their spiritual walk, and do they believe their church is well informed and has a good plan and vision for the future? I also wanted to know how much disparity there is between what their leaders believe is happening and what is actually occurring among the youth.

Getting unbiased answers to these questions isn't easy. Opinions are widely varied, and clearly the list of people interviewed could easily skew the results. To avoid personal bias, I asked several men from different conservative Anabaptist constituencies to contact church leaders and youth in their areas and create a list of possible interviewees. My hope was that by disconnecting myself from the selection process the results would be more accurate and representative of the larger group. To further avoid partiality, I asked that they work within certain parameters while gathering candidates.

1. I asked them to select a ratio of one older adult or church leader to two youth from each church community. There might be more variation among the youth than the adults, and I wanted to get a fair representation.

2. They were to ask the leaders for names of "average" young people within their church. I didn't want their shining stars, and neither did I want those who have major struggles with technology. I felt this segment of a youth group might be more objective.

3. My goal was to traverse the entire spectrum of conservative Anabaptist churches, from those that have consistently said no to technological advances to ones that seem to have little fear of electronic gadgetry but still view themselves as conservative.

Suppositions and Surprises

In the next few chapters we will look at the results of these interviews, but first I want to say this. All of us have thoughts on this topic. We have pondered this issue for many years and some of our opinions are quite strong. I am one of those people, and I went into these interviews with certain presuppositions. I have listened to arguments over the years, drawn conclusions, and formulated viewpoints. And while some of my assumptions were validated, I was unprepared for some of what I heard in these interviews, primarily in two areas.

First, I was shocked at the amount of questionable, and even immoral, content being consumed. Whether in short, supposedly funny video clips, movies, or outright pornography, electronic technology is exposing conservative Anabaptists to an incredible amount of sinful material. All of us have seen the statistics, but I was under an illusion that we were more removed from this than we are.

Second, it was apparent that many of our church leaders are not taking the threat of technology seriously enough. Many admit they are largely unprepared for the future. Conservative Anabaptist church fellowships, conferences, and local churches have slowly developed methods to dispense with issues that threaten the church community. Trial and error have shown what procedures work. Like a well-balanced engine, the church order in some groups has worked smoothly for years and seemed capable of handling any threat. But the infrastructure that worked for the threats of the 1950s isn't suited to the modern era.

Insufficient Infrastructure

Those first British engineers who proposed a subway system under London were more brilliant than they realized. As the city grew, many must have marveled at their foresight. History had proven them correct; the subway was a superb idea, but things have changed. The same tunnels, cut just large enough to get the trains through and designed perfectly for the early 1900s, are no longer working so well. The world has changed, but the size of the tunnels hasn't, and the infrastructure that was sufficient a hundred years ago is no longer adequate. I believe the same is true in many of our Anabaptist churches.

CHAPTER TWENTY

JUST SAY NO

Sitting down and discussing technology with "Daniel"[a] was enjoyable. He lives in a beautiful rural setting, has a large family, owns a dairy farm, and is the bishop of his local congregation. Daniel's horse and buggy fellowship has historically taken a very dim view of innovations, yet I found him transparent and willing to discuss this pressing issue. In Daniel's church, only phones with cords are allowed. Recently they have tried allowing business owners to have basic cell phones as long as they do not carry the phone with them during the day. Building contractors, for example, are supposed to leave their phones in their vehicles at work. But this restriction has brought another set of difficulties for their leaders.

"This happens all the time," Daniel said in exasperation. "Someone calls me to report that they saw one of our members carrying a cell phone at a jobsite. I am supposed to chase all these reports down, and this is creating a lot of work for the ministry." He explained that this issue has created much upheaval in their churches and some

---

[a] All names and some details from personal interviews have been changed to protect those who shared.

have even been excommunicated.

Daniel went on to describe their approach to the Internet. Their official position is that anything capable of accessing the Internet is forbidden. While at first this position sounds clear and simple, Daniel admitted there is controversy within their fellowship over what this means. Almost all their businesses are using programs that technically are not allowed, and owners have become adept at finding loopholes that are ignored by the leadership.

John is in Daniel's church, and his business is just down the road. Walking into his showroom is like walking into any secular business in America. In fact, other than the plain dress of the men behind the counter, nothing indicates a reluctance to embrace the world. Sitting down in John's tastefully decorated office, I couldn't help but notice the computers, copy machines, and other electronic gadgets. It was hard to imagine that John was in good standing in a fellowship that has excommunicated members for using a cell phone. So as we sat down in his private office, I asked John how this is possible.

"This is a huge issue in our church right now. There was a rule put in place last year that members of our church aren't allowed to even work on a computer that has Internet access. That made it really hard for people who aren't working for one of our people. Some have had to quit their jobs."

"But John, how can you be in the same church as these members who have had to leave their jobs, and yet have all this technology?"

John explained how their system works. Businessmen have found several ways to creatively bypass the rules. Some of them gain access to the Internet through one of their employees who is not a member of their church. If the Internet account isn't in the name of a church member, leaders tend to look the other way. Others have gone into partnership with someone from a more lenient church fellowship, and the Internet is then acceptable since the business isn't totally controlled by one of their members. In John's situation, he has salesmen and outside representatives who update his computers each time they visit. "We do have our own email account," John confessed, "and I think that is technically forbidden."

Those Who Say No

Daniel and John belong to one of many conservative fellowships that have historically just said no. They have viewed new inventions with a high level of suspicion and been slow to embrace change. As I listened to individuals from these constituencies, there were some things I admired.

These groups are being honest about the danger. Their reluctance to immediately follow the flow has given them time to examine negative outcomes in less restrictive groups. Some of them have prosperous farms, and there seems little need for additional exposure to technology. But there are also some obvious problems.

A Focus on Circumvention

In the interviews I conducted with individuals from groups who have tended to "just say no," there was a strong preoccupation with their group's standards. Consequently, they become adept and creative in achieving the objective (using the needed technology) while circumventing the rules that prohibit it. Rather than assessing each use of technology against Biblical principle, rules are made to restrict assimilation into culture. The primary response from members seems to be, "How can we still get the job done without disobeying this rule?" The result is tired leadership. Instead of guiding spiritually, many of them are busy trying to hold the line against the constant flood of innovations and individuals finding loopholes. The rule, not the Scriptural principle, becomes the focus. "Is he or isn't he complying with the church's standard?" is the issue, and the weightier issues tend to be forgotten. The benefit of this approach is that it is slowing their assimilation into culture in some situations.

Different Expectations for Youth

While there are exceptions, especially in smaller isolated groups, constituencies that are extremely slow to embrace change tend to have radically different expectations for members than they do for youth who have not yet joined the church. It was common for individuals to begin to answer a question, pause, and then ask, "Did you mean for our members or non-members?" There were distinctly different expectations.

Because of this, many of these communities provide very little, if any, teaching for their unconverted youth. Young people jump into technology with little understanding, guidance, or comprehension of the long-term damage of unfiltered Internet. Social media, ungodly movies, and pornography are common in many of the groups I met with. One young man said, "In some cases the parents try to keep us from it, but there really isn't much they can do." An Amish father told me he had taught his children from little up that Amish don't use the Internet. Then, while visiting the sale barn, his children suddenly realized their father wasn't up to date. Sitting in front of them were Amish youth accessing all kinds of websites on their phones. They watched as these youth took pictures and posted them on social media. Their father was shocked, and his children decided that their father was out of step with the times.

This heartbroken father went on to share how technology continues to impact his children. In his local area there are three categories of non-member youth. First is a smaller group of youth who are largely obedient and wouldn't own personal phones out of respect to their parents. Second are youth who don't drink, but have phones capable of accessing the Internet. Some of these have even met their future spouses on social media. Third are youth who seem to be rejecting everything Amish.

"In the past," this father told me, "most of the young people in this third group eventually came back to their roots. But that is changing, and many of these are no longer returning. Instead they are finding more liberal churches where they can continue using the technology they have become used to." This discouraged father has children in this third group.

The devastating spiritual impact on young people who are exposed to unfiltered Internet at an early age is immeasurable. Ironically, some of the worst situations are within these groups who are still attempting to "just say no." Because using the Internet is against their rules, these churches have little or no teaching on this issue.

Not only is this having a devastating effect on the older rebellious youth involved, but due to the portability of these devices, older youth bring them home and young children are accessing ungodly sites and developing an appetite for sinful material. Parents who wouldn't think of allowing a television into their home are looking the other way as their children's young minds are polluted by the same material viewed on a smartphone. Out of convenience, some parents also use the devices their children have purchased.

Part of this is due to ignorance. One father said that many Amish parents believe Facebook is just a harmless bulletin board for news. One Amish father told me, "Parents need to educate themselves. I went on Facebook through a coworker's account and was horrified at what I saw on my children's pages. I wish I hadn't seen it!" Some are not aware that pornography can be accessed so easily. Most see these gadgets as just another toy that is acceptable for nonmembers to play with. As one unconcerned parent said, "This is just like other things we have had to deal with in the past." Unfortunately, many are finding out it isn't at all like anything we have seen before.

The Church: Unable to Address Cultural Reality

One question I asked each person I interviewed was, "How confident are you that your church will be able to handle the coming onslaught of technology?" While I didn't find anyone who was extremely confident, there was obviously less confidence on the conservative end of the spectrum. There may be several explanations for this, but one obvious reason is the lack of proactive thought in these groups. Many of them, by their own admission, tend to react to issues rather than prayerfully planning. In the past, just being suspicious of innovations has worked well. But many in these groups are alarmed. One spoke of just being in "survival mode," and another said, "When I look at our community, I feel like we're a ship without a rudder!"

This is especially alarming to young people with active minds. They see their leaders saying no without taking the time to research or find alternatives. One young conservative Mennonite business owner spoke of the frustration of decisions regarding technology being made by older men whose financial futures are secure. Their land is paid for, they don't need the Internet, and they see no reason to allow exceptions. Meanwhile, some of the younger men are trying to start small businesses and compete with companies whose use of technology is unrestricted. In addition, within their fellowship they see widespread use of technology below the radar. They get a sense that their leaders are not only disregarding current business realities, but also underestimating the spiritual danger. Perhaps most damaging is the effect this is having on how young people see the church—impotent, irrelevant, and inwardly focused.

Is It All About Us?

I want people to think well of me, and it is easy to act religious, use spiritual lingo, and be involved in all manner of good things. It is also possible for all this to be about me. The same is true for our churches. It is easy for a church to become enamored with preserving its own image rather than pursuing the image of Christ. Are we burdened by the issues that weigh on the heart of God, or does our concern with problems like technology center around ourselves and how we are perceived by other congregations? Are we giving thought to how our decisions impact the integration of serious seekers within our community?

When the Holy Spirit works within the heart of an unbeliever, He draws the person not just to Himself, but also into a church family. God is at work in the lives of men and women all around us, and as He works, they begin to seek answers and fellowship. But I found very little interest in connecting with these people within the "just say no" groups that I interviewed. One bishop told me he had never seen an "outsider" join his church within his lifetime. This didn't totally surprise me, but what I found most disconcerting was the nonchalant way he said it. The fact that his church seemed incapable of integrating seekers didn't seem of concern. This was consistent among the extremely cautious groups. None seemed too concerned that their standards were arbitrary or unexplainable to someone raised outside their fellowship. It didn't seem to bother them that their fellowship is unattainable for the serious seeker from the secular community.

"It's Just Not Working!"

This chapter is a brief overview of the segment of conservative Anabaptists who tend to just say no, and admittedly the picture has often not been pretty. However, there are those within these fellowships who have maintained good relationships with their children and successfully steered them through the maze of electronic gadgetry. As one Amish father told me, "There are families among us that do not have smartphones due to good relationships with their children and good teaching. But this is rare!"

This chapter began with an interview of dairy farmer Daniel, the bishop who was weary of chasing down reports of infractions. As I prepared to leave his farm, I asked, "Daniel, if you were writing a book on technology, what would your focus be?" He looked out across the field and pondered the question before responding. "I would focus on how we should be dealing with it, because we can't deny it is here. This thing of just restricting everything sounds good, but it's just not working!"

I don't believe he was saying that the answer was to stop saying no. If we are going to survive what is coming, we will need to reject specific uses of technologies. This bishop was saying that his group needs to do *more* than just say no. Beyond rejecting devices, they need a stronger emphasis on teaching Biblical principle, developing spiritual life, and building relationships within the church.

CHAPTER TWENTY-ONE

JUST FOCUS ON BIBLICAL PRINCIPLE

Melvin is a serious-minded father of five. He operates a local cabinet shop and has an obvious love for the Lord, a likeable personality, and a passion for the Word of God. Melvin was raised in a horse-and-buggy community, and as a young man he became concerned about the spiritual apathy within his church. Like the churches that we considered in the last chapter, his local leaders tended to "just say no" to every new thing that came along. Yet these restrictions didn't bother Melvin as much as the hypocrisy and lack of spiritual interest. People seemed to care much more about compliance with church rules than having a genuine relationship with God. Over time, he began to view the focus on rules as the problem. He longed for a church where each member had an inner spiritual walk with God rather than being held in check by outer regulations. Eventually Melvin left his community and joined a fellowship where the inner life was emphasized, and today he is a pastor in this church.

Like Melvin, many leaders have taken the "just focus on principle" approach in their fellowships. They have reacted to "dead legalism" and are attempting to work from within rather than enforcing from without. But as I listened to these leaders share their concerns, most are not comfortable with the results. After explaining their approach, Melvin made this observation.

> With our current level of accountability and the church model we have, I'm not overly confident. We do church for two hours on Sunday morning, and maybe one and a half hours Wednesday night. My congregation, unfortunately, is spending more time in front of a screen than they are listening to our teaching. One of our men recently confessed that he hasn't picked up his Bible in two weeks. I'm afraid that may be more common than we like to admit. Other pastors are hearing the same thing.

Pastors in this group are not interested in going back to dead formalism and a focus on rules, but neither are they confident that their present methods are effective. Most are certain they are losing ground but unsure what to do. This is the other end of the spectrum from the "just say no" fellowships, and there are some points they tend to emphasize.

Emphasize Scriptural Truth
One of the oft-repeated refrains from these fellowships is the importance of relying on the Word of God and teaching Scriptural principle. They focus heavily on teaching, seminars, and good sermons packed with excellent content, and this is bearing good fruit in their members. But they have a problem. How can they compete with electronic entertainment? When the minds of your congregation are captivated throughout the week by humorous videos, engaging news clips, and fascinating documentaries, how can you produce a message capable of holding their attention?

Almost every modern church is dealing with a similar problem.

Even people in churches that have banned electronics are consuming books and reading newspapers. More time is spent receiving information from outside sources than from a Sunday sermon. But there is a major difference, as we saw earlier, between receiving information from a printed page versus an animated screen. This was Melvin's concern. How is a minister supposed to meet the needs of a congregation that consumes entertainment during the week and has become used to that level of stimuli?

Dialogue, but Don't Make Decisions
While most individuals within "just focus on Biblical principle" churches are fearful of collective agreements, they are not opposed to dialogue. Several mentioned the importance of sharing and talking about the challenges of technology within a group setting. Bible studies, retreats, and other programs facilitate more discussion. Some described times when individuals have confessed improper use of technology and asked for additional accountability. Cell groups are being used in some churches so members can share struggles in a smaller setting, and almost every leader had a story of someone who had found victory. "Confess your faults one to another, and pray one for another, that ye may be healed,"[a] was a common theme. Building relationships and continual dialogue seemed to be the goals and primary weapons of this group. Of course, this takes a tremendous amount of time, and most leaders confessed that this was not happening as it should.

Relegate the Issue to Fathers
Paul is in his sixties and was born into an Amish community. He talked about growing up in a "legalistic environment," a setting where rules without relationship were predominant. After marriage, he left the Amish, joined a church with a more spiritual focus, and then a few years later he moved on to an even more progressive fellowship. It has now been over forty years, yet he is still heavily

---
[a] James 5:16

impacted by the hypocrisy he encountered in his youth. Today he is a pastor, and as I listened, this theme of "no rules" seemed predominant. Yet he understands the need for some technology guidelines. His leaders have decided to transfer this responsibility to the fathers. "Our church constitution says that we strongly encourage fathers to monitor and make decisions for their home with regard to technology. So if our leadership tried to take control of that area, we would be in violation of our own standards."

Relegating decision-making to the family was a consistent theme from individuals who have been burnt in the past by rules without relationship. An emphasis is placed on the father's role in the home, and these churches try to provide frequent exhortation to their men, encouraging them to take their role seriously. Of course, regardless of a church's position, every father should take his charge seriously. God gave specific instructions to fathers throughout the Bible, reminding them that training their children is their responsibility. But what about the widow who is trying to provide direction to her teenage son? Or what happens when a father doesn't take his proper place in the home? What about the impact children who are constantly being exposed to Hollywood might have on other youth in a congregation?

I spoke with the principal of an Anabaptist Christian day school. This school has children from various denominations, and he shared some challenges technology is bringing to their classrooms. "I have children who come to me and say that they are concerned about what their parents are watching. Some of them have subscriptions to Netflix and download secular movies on a regular basis."

These children know from what they are learning at church and school that something is wrong with what their parents are doing. But what can leaders do if the church has relegated all responsibility for digital consumption to the parents? How can they rescue the children? Is that even their responsibility? Leaders who have transferred all decisions regarding technology to fathers have to wrestle with these questions.

Hope for the Best

Leaders within churches that focus on principle but are skittish about rules do not seem to be more confident than leaders who just say no. Many of them are wringing their hands and just hoping for the best. While this group tends to do better in building relationships and providing good teaching, they also have youth who are struggling.

Sharon is seventeen and has an engaging and outgoing personality. When she walked into the room, I was immediately impressed by her calm demeanor, friendly smile, and modest appearance. Sharon belongs to a "just focus on principle" church, and as I asked questions about her personal use of technology, the word that came to mind was "casual." Sharon is in almost constant communication with friends on various social media platforms, enjoys sharing trending videos, and fills any quiet time with contemporary music. When her youth group meets, it is often to watch the latest movie or a popular television program together. When I asked Sharon how she decides which movies are appropriate, she replied, "Probably based on ratings. If the show is rated "R," then it will depend on why it got that rating. Most of the movies we watch are rated PG-13."

After a day of interviewing youth in "just focus on principle" churches, I told my wife, "The hardest part of this project is keeping my eyebrows level while listening to these young people." I knew that a surprised facial expression would halt discussion. How do you suppress alarm when a young woman who professes to follow the Lord has such a nonchalant view of electronic media? Someone should be alarmed! Sharon is a lovely young girl with an honest desire to serve the Lord, but it is impossible for youth to constantly consume our culture's entertainment and come out unscathed. Yet, is Sharon really at fault here? I had the opportunity to interview one of Sharon's pastors as well. Notice his responses to specific questions regarding technology.

Q: "Describe how your youth use smartphones."

A: "We probably don't have a good handle on it. I have just left this in the hands of the fathers to decide what they are comfortable with."

Q: "What about movies?"

A: "I suppose it does happen some. How much, I don't know."

Q: "How much specific teaching/warning takes place in your congregation regarding electronic entertainment?"

A: "Specific teaching would not be very common."

Is it any wonder that the youth in this church are heavily involved in electronic entertainment?

After interviewing Sharon's pastor, the same word came to mind. Casual. Both seem to have a carefree attitude regarding the impact of electronic media and culture. I wondered about their youth group. Where will Sharon and her friends be in twenty years? She is a very nice girl, but will she survive the tech tsunami? Is this a one-generation approach? Many leaders in these churches freely confess they aren't sure they are on the right path. They are losing many of their youth to the world but aren't sure what steps to take.

Some families within this segment seem to be doing well. The church isn't taking much of a position, so parents are attempting to keep the hearts of their children. However, their children are often in youth groups that are heavily involved in electronic entertainment. Most of the youth in these groups, by their own admission, are not doing well.

We Can't Find Reverse

One of the questions I asked everyone I interviewed was: "If your church decided to back up and use less technology, how would your members respond?" In other words, regardless of the current level of usage, could you reduce that level? Remember, I was interviewing people across a wide spectrum. Some wouldn't use a basic cell phone, while others sponsored youth group movie nights. Yet each person's response, regardless of age or position in the church, was similar. Few individuals believed their community could reverse the course. When a fellowship accepts a specific technology, it becomes almost impossible to back up. Once we get accustomed to a convenience, whether it is listening to a cappella singing on the telephone or having access to unfiltered Internet on personal devices, it is difficult to accept additional restrictions. If rules about technology are imposed in a conservative congregation, the problem tends to go underground. If they're implemented in progressive congregations, attendees often move to another church.

There are exceptions. Churches that place a premium on close relationships and purposely and frequently reassess their vision can make changes and back up when outcomes are not what they desire. But most fellowships seem to have difficulty reversing technology.

Why Is It So Difficult?

Most church leaders I interviewed who have put all their hopes on good teaching are not seeing the fruit they would like. Most of these men had left settings they considered legalistic, and their hope was that an abundance of sound Biblical exegesis would offset the influence of electronic media. Their goal was relationship without rules. Several are actively pouring themselves into building relationships among their youth, and they are doing the best. But most find it hard to compete with constant access to engaging and exciting media.

One pastor concluded our time together by saying, "We are not prepared to handle the future. We haven't put enough energy into it." He paused before walking out the door. "Sometimes I ask myself, why is it so difficult to back up from these things we know are a detriment to us?"

CHAPTER TWENTY-TWO

TECHNOLOGY AND OUR CONCEPT OF CHURCH

The two basic approaches to technology we looked at in the last two chapters represent the two extremes among conservative Anabaptists I interviewed. It wouldn't be fair to place every congregation within these two categories. Yet, as I listened to a wide variety of church leaders and youth, patterns began to develop, and I realized that the issue is much greater than just how churches are dealing with technology. It goes back to how a fellowship chooses to "do church."

In this chapter I would like to share some observations. I have labeled churches by models of administration, but remember that no church or fellowship fits perfectly into just one model. Within the churches I will describe, individual members may well fit better in another model. That is both the challenge of categorizing and the beauty of the church.

Even though there is crossover, I saw enough patterns to persuade me that certain approaches to church government produce consistent results. Again, there are exceptions, but with this disclaimer, let's walk through four basic approaches—permissive, regulated, intellectual, and integrated—and observe their outcomes.

Permissive Approach

Churches in this category exhibit little difference from the "seeker-friendly" evangelical churches that surround them. In fact, other than some remaining vestiges from their Anabaptist past, they seem to be moving toward mainstream Christianity. The individuals I

Permissive Approach	**Little Focus on Biblical Teaching** **Little Commitment to Church Community**
Role of Leaders	Entertaining worship—administer ordinances
Relationship between members	Weak accountability—avoidance of conflict
How youth see church	Both Biblical and in tune with culture
Posture toward acculturation	Little attempt to address
Impact of technology	Overwhelmed by entertainment & social media
Seekers	Only attractive to those with low expectations

interviewed who would fit here are very interested in fulfilling the "felt needs" of the congregation and seekers. Some of them had experienced ecclesiastical abuse and grown up with church leaders who focused more on enforcing rules than on guiding their people's hearts. In churches taking the permissive approach, the worship services are intended to be uplifting, and they occasionally use multi-media presentations in their Sunday morning services. They would be opposed to any type of church guidelines and prefer to leave specific application to the family. Regarding the threat of technology, one pastor told me "I think the church should be focusing on proper teaching, training, and understanding about the good stuff." When I asked him how often this happens, he said, "We had a guy in a year ago or so for a weekend of meetings on media. Other than that, we don't talk about it much."

I also interviewed some of the youth from his congregation. A few of these young men have had difficult battles with pornography, and one of them made this observation. "I get into it for a while and then get back out. Sometimes I think I have conquered it, but then it comes back. I feel unsupported by my pastor. It would help a lot to have an accountability group. I wouldn't want my son to experience what I have gone through." He has tried talking to his pastor about it, but senses that his pastor doesn't understand how difficult the battle is. I prayed with this young man and tried to encourage him. My heart was heavy as I watched him walk out the door. Will he survive in this permissive church with a casual approach to technology?

Regulated Approach

We looked at this model in the chapter "Just Say No." The regulated approach is on the opposite end of the spectrum from the permissive approach. Yet I was struck at how similar the results were among the youth. Youth in a permissive church tend to see their church

Regulated Approach	Little Focus on Biblical Teaching Strong Commitment to Church Community
Role of Leaders	Maintain and enforce baseline rules
Relationship between members	Individuals are held by church culture
How youth see church	Fearful of open dialogue—lacks forward vision
Posture toward acculturation	Preoccupation with baseline rules
Impact of technology	Hidden usage—focus on creative circumvention
Seekers	Drawn to lifestyle—integration extremely difficult

following the world, while the youth in a highly regulated church feel their church is simply reacting to the world. Most young people appreciated their church's caution but longed for more opportunities to talk and share their struggles. Several mentioned a lack of applicable teaching. Some who became ensnared by immoral content during their teens found little support and had difficulty recovering.

Many youth in regulated churches plunge from almost no exposure to the "outside" during childhood into total cultural immersion in their teenage years. Because they are not supposed to have access to electronics, they have had little teaching on the dangers, and handheld technology offers them access to unimaginable evil. In some cases, parents are aware that their children are exposed to immorality, but they have little comprehension of the long-term consequences. Many youth become heavily involved before joining the church and are scarred for life.

The impact this is having on plain communities cannot be overstated. In 2015 a group of deeply concerned Old Order Amish leaders published a small booklet titled "A Wake-Up Call." In this little booklet the writer sounded a sober alarm. "We have a serious concern that these little devices will accomplish what fire, water, and sword failed to do."[1]

Most churches using the regulated approach give little thought to seekers in their neighborhoods. Rules are created to avoid acculturation, and then additional rules are created to offset the deficiencies. Over time, this develops into a tangle of seemingly arbitrary rules difficult to unravel, especially for anyone who wasn't born within the culture. Consequently, few outsiders seek for God within highly regulated churches. When they do, it rarely provides long-term satisfaction for either the seeker or the church.

Intellectual Approach

While the regulated approach leans heavily on structure, the intellectual approach has a strong emphasis on Biblical exegesis. Sermons

Intellectual Approach	Strong Focus on Biblical Teaching Little Commitment to Church Community
Role of Leaders	Biblical teachers—well-presented lectures
Relationship between members	Coexist—tolerate differences
How youth see church	Leaders fearful of addressing specifics in culture
Posture toward acculturation	Little specific teaching—fear of agreements
Impact of technology	Continual drift toward entertainment
Seekers	Attracted by expository preaching

are thoughtful, well-crafted expository presentations, and ministers usually give much thought to word studies and carefully unpacking the Word of God verse by verse. Church tends to be a place where solid Biblical messages are delivered each Lord's Day. But in some of these churches, there is a major difference between the emphasis on personal holiness in sermons and the reality found in the lives of members. One young individual who listens to these excellent weekly expositions told me, "If our ministers knew what all is going on, I don't think they would be comfortable." Movies, humorous YouTube videos, and even television network streaming among the youth is common in this individual's congregation. The leaders express concern, but many don't have a grasp on what is happening during the week. Their hope is that a continual focus on the Word of God will eventually turn the tide and win this battle. Unfortunately, it is hard for a one-hour message, regardless of its power, to compete with constant electronic bombardment.

As in all the church models, I did find a few bright spots in these congregations. Some have become convicted by the Holy Spirit, communicated with others in the group who are likeminded, and set up accountability groups. This is voluntary and can create a group-within-the-group effect, but one must applaud their effort. One young lady who would like to see the leaders take a more active role told me she believes they want to lead; they just aren't sure how.

I talked to many young people who long for leaders brave enough to come together and prayerfully discuss specific ways their church could be more proactive. Some expressed a desire to see their entire fellowship band together, prayerfully seek collective application, and decide on some basic agreements to guide their daily lives. These churches have godly leaders who would like to build better relationships with the youth and at times wonder if a few boundaries might be helpful. But there is tremendous fear of heading down that road and being viewed as legalistic.

Integrated Approach

After interviewing multiple individuals in churches overrun with

Integrated Approach	Strong Focus on Biblical Teaching Strong Commitment to Church Community
Role of Leaders	Biblical teachers—focus on applications of doctrine
Relationship between members	Members lovingly hold each other accountable
How youth see church	More powerful than culture
Posture toward acculturation	Clear teaching—willing to draw lines if needed
Impact of technology	Used as a tool for occupations and outreach
Seekers	Drawn by teaching and obvious sacrificial love

electronic entertainment, I became discouraged at times. *Is anything actually working? Have we totally underestimated this electronic monster?* Then a clear-eyed young man would walk in and share his experience.

Thomas is eighteen and enjoys technology. He carries a smartphone and works on computers in his spare time. Interestingly, even with constant exposure to electronic media, Thomas has never watched a secular movie. He is one of many young people out there who are not only surviving but thriving in our current environment. This hasn't happened by accident, and there are some common denominators behind these young people. They have older members behind them who are actively engaged and taking serious steps to ensure success. They are not refusing to use technology or assuming that teaching will be sufficient. Thomas's church is constantly rethinking their position and prayerfully seeking workable solutions. Thomas has gained tremendous insight from his leaders. "I've heard people say, if the heart is right nothing else matters," he told me. "But I believe if the heart is right, everything else matters. If your heart is right, you are going to want to control things like technology."

> If the heart is right, everything matters.

One young lady belongs to a congregation where the leadership takes an active and comprehensive role in protecting their youth. She frequently uses a computer, but her activity is constantly monitored and reported to an older accountability partner. "I know better than to go on some sites. Just knowing that someone will know if I do is a great help." She has the normal curiosity of a young person, but she sees accountability as a blessing. She went on to say that she sees her church as a leader in this area. She lives in confidence that her leaders are actively thinking, developing battle strategies, and planning ahead. Youth in integrated approach churches talked about the blessing of knowing their leaders have frequent discussions on this topic. One young man noted that the men in his congregation frequently discuss ways to protect each other. He likes that he is surrounded by men who are serious about this subject. Another young man, whose father is a leader in his church, said his family has frequent discussions around the dinner table about technology and how it is being used. These are young people who feel cared for and are not left alone in the battle.

I have labeled this an integrated approach rather than a moderate approach for a reason. These churches understand the fallacy of believing that rules alone will solve this issue. Neither have they fallen for the belief that good teaching by itself will suffice. Rather, an integrated approach seeks to encompass both. But make no mistake. This approach isn't easy, and a word of warning here is essential. It might be tempting to assume that some occasional teaching, a few rules, and a little accountability will be enough. I want to be clear—few churches that I am aware of are doing well in handling technology. If we are going to effectively implement an integrated approach, it will require much Biblical teaching accompanied with a high level of accountability. Churches that are successfully navigating technological change are pouring much energy into this area. They have ongoing discussions, collective prayer, and a keen focus on building strong relationships within the brotherhood. They understand that each member faces different temptations, and they are willing to restrict personal liberties for the good of their weaker brother.[a]

Congregations taking the integrated approach are not all part of one denomination. Neither do they all fit within one stratum of conservatism. Yet there are enough similarities that we should note the common denominators.

Concluding Observations

There is risk in trying to establish categories, and no church I have seen fits squarely within one of these models. So many dynamics exist within any one congregation that it wouldn't be fair to place it into only one of these categories. Yet we can learn important things from this exercise, and the models were helpful as I tried to process what I was hearing from leaders and youth.

I wish I could say that most of our churches are doing well—that leadership is taking the challenge of electronic entertainment seriously, and youth are learning to prayerfully discern. I would like to report that most of our churches are fasting regarding this issue, and that most of us are prayerfully seeking "a right way for us, and for our little ones."[b] It would be wonderful to report that we have an abundance of men like the "children of Issachar, which were men that had understanding of the times, to know what Israel ought to do."[c] Unfortunately, too many of us are taking a simplistic approach to technology. Either we adopt the one-dimensional "just say no" approach, or we assume the occasional warning is enough. Electronic technology is not just a spot of rough water the church must navigate; it is a virtual tsunami. Failure to recognize its influence is having

> Electronic technology is not just a spot of rough water the church must navigate; it is a virtual tsunami.

---

[a] Romans 14:1–21; 1 Corinthians 10:23–33
[b] Ezra 8:21
[c] 1 Chronicles 12:32

a devastating impact, both on our personal lives and our churches.

Several reoccurring themes emerge among churches that are doing well. I believe it is worthwhile to reiterate them.

1. Their leaders take the challenge of electronic technology seriously and pour energy into solutions and Biblical teaching. They undergird all they do with a strong emphasis on the underlying Scriptural principle.

2. These churches understand the importance of building close relationships. They value transparency and ask each other hard questions. Some could quote the questions they regularly ask each other; they are actively and lovingly holding each other accountable.

3. They are not afraid to draw some lines for their congregation. They understand that agreements alone will never be enough. They know that rules without relationship have little positive power and can be ugly if taken to an extreme. Yet they are not afraid to prayerfully develop basic boundaries for their people.

These congregations are not taking this challenge lightly or assuming a simple solution will appear. But the challenge isn't keeping them from actively resisting. The stakes are simply too high to ignore the problem.

CHAPTER TWENTY-THREE

THE SCOURGE OF PORN

All of us are aware that pornography is readily available on the Internet. In fact, it is estimated that up to 30 percent of all data transferred across the Internet is pornography.[1] In 2018 a survey revealed that 43% of Americans now view pornography as morally acceptable. This is up 7% from just a year before.[2] Clearly, morality in America is shifting. Even more sobering, pastors are not immune to this scourge. In a 2016 survey of American pastors, 57 percent confessed to a current or past struggle with pornography, and 64 percent of youth pastors confessed seeking it out.[3] Many sermons, seminars, and books have been produced addressing this epidemic. Of course, these figures are only estimates. Those involved are not proud of their activity and keep it hidden. Consequently, gathering accurate numbers is difficult at best.

These are astounding statistics, and it is difficult to wrap my mind around the percentages. When I was young, accessing this kind of trash would have meant walking into a store, selecting a porn magazine, and facing the cashier. I suspected some people were willing to do that, but probably no one I knew. Recently I was on an airplane flying into an Asian country where a high percentage of men arriving come to seek prostitutes. As the plane descended, I looked around the cabin. Most passengers were men, and all of them looked like upstanding citizens. Most were dressed in business suits, and I couldn't imagine any of them fitting into this category. Yet according to the statistics, some must. I have the same problem grasping that pastors are involved in pornography. I am aware that American Christianity has washed out on many major doctrines. I know holiness is no longer a major focus in many churches, yet I have trouble visualizing leaders who stand up and proclaim God's word each Sunday while secretly looking at pornographic material through the week.

Maybe that explains why I was unprepared for what I found when interviewing conservative Anabaptists. I went into this project knowing that pornography exists, that a large percentage of men are involved, and conservative Anabaptists are made of the same stuff as everyone else. Yet looking back, I realize I had subconsciously assumed we were a little superior.

It's Everywhere!

Eli was a young Amish country boy, as far removed from technology as a young man in America can be. One day he was walking along the road, picking up aluminum cans, when he spied a pornographic magazine someone had thrown out of a car window. That brief exposure started Eli on a downward journey and impacted his life in ways he could have never anticipated. A fire was ignited within him that has never totally died out. Today he is over thirty and still struggling. He has accessed pornography on flip phones, smartphones, and computers. He, like many young men, has wondered if something is wrong with him. "Is it a chemical imbalance?" he asked me. "Is my situation just different than other men? Sometimes I wonder if this is stronger in me than most other men." Eli was raised in a home where technology was shunned, yet Satan found a way in.

Tim's story is different. His parents gave little thought to the danger of technology. They assumed the best about their children and failed to consider cultural risk. Tim's path to pornography began with a car magazine. He was only eight years old, but those scantily clad models stirred his curiosity. He began to look for pictures in catalogs and other publications, and when he was thirteen he discovered online pornography. His parents had unfiltered Internet in their home, and Tim became deeply involved with porn sites. For seven years he secretly accessed pornography within his home. Outwardly, he lived an upright life. He was involved with his youth group, and his parents had a high opinion of him. Occasionally Tim would even overhear one of them talking about their wonderful son. He knew he needed help, but he wasn't sure where to turn. Tim was addicted to porn but afraid to disappoint his parents by telling them.

Deliverance
Both Eli and Tim eventually sought help. Their church communities operate very differently, but they found older men who were willing to listen, pray with them, and walk with them toward restoration. But it hasn't been easy. Both young men shared their painful path to recovery.

Eli's community doesn't allow Internet access, and their answer has been to impose additional restrictions. His Amish leaders have focused primarily on monitoring his activities and his time away from home.

Tim's church has taken a different approach. His parents have been his primary resource. They have encouraged him toward spiritual growth and spending time in the Word of God. They haven't restricted his access to the Internet but have tried to hold him accountable with frequent questions. Tim credits their loving influence in his success in overcoming his addiction. Though both men would say they have made progress, neither would say the battle is over. In fact, each has a serious message he would like to share with his church, but neither is sure how to convey his deep concern.

The Battle Rages On!
Eli is a naturally quiet young man, but he came alive when privately

discussing this topic. "People assume I am over it. I did have someone ask me how I was doing a while back, but it is very rare. They don't ask like I wish they would!" Eli went on to say that at first everyone was concerned and many tried to help. "People kind of backed off after a while. I wish they would keep asking and holding me accountable. There is still a stronger battle inside me than people realize."

Tim's community is much more open regarding issues like this, and he has tremendous appreciation for the effort his parents and church leaders poured into his situation. As time passes, however, people assume that the battle is over. Tim's parents now have a filter on their Internet, and over time they have provided less personal accountability. His church leaders are busy men, and they have moved on to more pressing issues. Tim wishes he could describe to those who have never experienced the devastating power of pornography how difficult it is to recover. He would like for them to grasp, even in a small way, the ongoing intensity of the battle. His parents and leaders have moved on. For Tim, the daily battle continues.

When I began interviewing young people, I hadn't planned to ask if they had ever accessed online pornography themselves. But as young men, and some older ones, began voluntarily sharing their struggles with pornography, I began to ask all the men. The consistent theme from those who have struggled is how long and difficult the path to recovery is, and how their church leaders underestimate continued accountability. Some of these young people are crying out for someone to walk with them. They feel internally damaged and long for people who care enough to keep holding them accountable.

The Weakening of the Church

Jesus gave his disciples a sober warning about hypocrisy. "For there is nothing covered, that shall not be revealed; neither hid, that shall not be known. Therefore whatsoever ye have spoken in darkness shall be heard in the light; and that which ye have spoken in the ear in closets shall be proclaimed upon the housetops."[a]

I thought of these words while going back over these interviews. Even though we know that millions of people are accessing pornography at any given moment, how often have you observed someone involved? I see people all the time using the Internet in coffee shops, offices, or airports. Yet I don't recall ever seeing someone openly viewing pornography. Why? Because it is almost always done in secret. There is still shame involved, even for unbelievers. Make no mistake, the result of this type of sin, regardless of how well we hide it, will be shouted from the housetops.

How much power have our churches lost due to pornography? How many believers have lost their close connection to God, their ability to pray fervently, or their ability to exhort fellow brothers and sisters because of this plague? How many honest seekers have become confused and lost their way due to unclear testimony from a professing believer hiding his addiction? You can't hide the spiritual lethargy in a church that is ravaged by pornography. It is time we take this attack from our adversary seriously.

---

[a] Luke 12:2, 3

CHAPTER TWENTY-FOUR

WHAT ARE WE LISTENING TO?

One of the most powerful ways electronic technology is impacting the church today is through recorded audio. Music has a tremendous influence on people. It has been used to calm those who are troubled and to rouse soldiers to bravery as they head into battle. It can also incite youth to rebel against authority. Music motivates the listener in ways he may not fully understand. It is a powerful force that has strongly influenced cultures throughout history. It also powerfully impacts the church today.

Music is a gift from God, and singing should be coming out of our lives, homes, and congregations. The Scripture is clear that followers of Jesus are to be a singing people. But singing isn't just something we are to do, it is also something we are to listen to. The Apostle Paul told the church at Colosse that they were to teach and admonish "one another in psalms and hymns and spiritual songs."[a] He intended that believers be strengthened, cautioned, and encouraged by the singing of others. At the time Paul sent this instruction

---

[a] Colossians 3:16

to the church, the listener needed to be near the singer.

In the modern day, even the most basic phones can record sound. Now we can listen to singing, sermons, audio books, or lectures on an almost endless variety of topics. And due to the portable nature of the devices capable of playing recordings, this can happen while we are working, driving, or sitting alone in our bedrooms. Technology gives us an amazing array of options and opportunities. What is the net result for the church today? It has been both a blessing and a curse, but let's begin with the blessing.

The Blessing of Audio

God is using recorded audio in many ways. I think of the many elderly who, due to loss of eyesight, are blessed by audio Bibles. Sitting alone, they can focus on eternal truths and promises of Scripture even though they are no longer able to read. At a time in life when discouragement can set in, they can listen to old hymns and their minds can be raised in thankfulness to God.

Beyond the elderly, think of the great blessing recorded audio has been to new converts. Some new followers of Jesus have lived very dark lives and have memories they would like to erase. Some have an immoral past or have had multiple marriages, and they now live alone and struggle with a sanctified thought life. Wholesome music, solid preaching, and hours of listening to the Word of God while they work are a great blessing to their spiritual lives. This is also a way for them to fight against the ungodly music they listened to for years.

Those of us who grew up in Christian homes and have attended church all our lives carry a huge catalog of memorized songs. When we gather for a meal or fellowship, often the entire group will join in singing from memory. Imagine how it feels to be a newcomer and have no idea what this song is or where to find it. The opportunity to learn from recorded audio is a great blessing for new converts trying to merge into conservative church life. It can speed up the transition and help them feel included.

I remember visiting a little shack in a third world slum. These people were new converts to a conservative group, and I tried to imagine raising a family in this setting. Rock music drifted in from the neighbors and angry shouts penetrated the rusty corrugated steel walls; periods of silence were rare in this neighborhood. These new believers didn't have the option of moving to a calm place in the country. Their best option was to drown out the noise with recorded gospel hymns. In settings like this, godly music can also be an excellent way to reach out to others.

I think of another time in a different country, walking through another very poor neighborhood. All around me were the signs of lost humanity—the smell of alcohol, the sound of arguments, the display of immodesty—but as I continued deeper into this impoverished community I heard some familiar, beautiful a cappella singing. I had never met these people, but someone had given these new believers a tool to push back against their culture. This simple tool was recorded audio.

The Challenge of Audio

Just as recorded audio can be a great blessing to a church, it can also be a powerful curse. The same technology that can encourage can be a detriment, and as I interviewed youths, I was sobered.

Most conservative churches have historically dealt with this issue by controlling devices, and this has been somewhat successful. After all, if you don't own a device that can play recorded audio, then it isn't an issue. The offshoot was that many churches neglected to teach spiritual discernment, especially in music. Why teach discernment when people don't have the device? Today, recorded music is available in an astounding array of formats. Young people who have received little training on spiritually discerning music are suffering for it. Satan is subtly using something that can be beautiful to destroy and undermine.

We Follow Our Heroes

As young people talked about using technology to listen to audio and shared their preferences in music, one point became clear. They know which groups or singers they like. A strong attachment builds between the listener and the performers. One church leader told me, "We worship with those we listen to." He went on to say that this attachment becomes so strong it is almost impossible to break. "I have seen young people walk away from friends, family, even their local church. But it is very rare to see someone leave their music." He added that listening to "Christian" music with different doctrinal beliefs can drastically affect a listener's theology.

> We worship with those we listen to.

If you use the radio and admire the logic of certain talk show hosts, it will subtly influence your own conclusions and decisions. If you enjoy listening to radio preachers, your theology will gradually shift. If you admire a singing group and sense that their music brings you closer to God, you will want to become more like them. We follow our heroes. Those on the album cover may dress in ways that directly defy God's Word. But if you find spiritual nourishment in their music, over time you will tend to rethink outward appearance. You may be aware that this group doesn't embrace Jesus' teaching on loving our enemies. But if your spirit connects to their music and you begin to admire them, you will eventually view some of these basic teachings of Jesus differently.

I recently visited an Anabaptist bookstore and found myself standing in front of the recorded music display. Many of the albums produced by conservative Anabaptist groups seemed to employ secular marketing techniques that fly in the face of what they represent. I believe this deserves some consideration.

Let's assume you are going to distribute a CD of a sermon given by your pastor. Would he be comfortable with a picture of himself on the cover, standing in front of your church, arms crossed and gazing confidently into the camera? Most pastors would recoil from this. After all, it is the message he wants to promote, not the messenger.

Then why are we comfortable making the group who produced the album the focal point on the cover? This isn't an attempt to shame groups who have put their picture on an album. Rather, we need to give thought to how we regard and use music. Do we really want to promote particular groups? Creating heroes can easily divert our focus from the music to the ones producing it.

Subtle Shift

Most groups accept recorded audio with the intent of blessing their people and reaching out to others. But listening appetites shift. Music affects our emotions, and we tend to follow what feels good. This imperceptible movement from music as worship to music as entertainment is an almost inevitable slide. This is sobering! I was amazed at how little discernment youth are exercising in their choices. I interviewed some who, just one generation ago, weren't even allowed to have recorded audio. Today, youth from these same churches are dabbling with ungodly music. How could they move so quickly? They started by allowing only recorded congregational singing, yet something shifted, and today they enjoy listening to someone croon seductively into the microphone.

I was disturbed by the number of youth in very conservative groups who toy with a wide range of music, both secular and Christian. One young girl saw no danger in what her youth group was listening to. "There are a lot of explicit songs out there in pop, but if you use your judgment there can be good songs in any genre." She went on to say that her youth group listens to just about everything—contemporary Christian, country, Christian rock, even secular rock—and she thought there was some good in all of it. Another youth echoed a common response when he said, "The older ones in my church would be surprised at what the youth are listening to. They probably know we are listening to some stuff that isn't that great, but they don't know the extent."

We Rarely Back Up

Another sobering fact is that recorded music, like other forms of technology we addressed earlier, seldom backs up. Once a device or type of recorded music is accepted, most groups have difficulty reverting. One of the questions I asked everyone was this: "What if your leaders decided your present use of audio wasn't blessing your congregation. Would your church be willing to back up?" Almost everyone said that it would be almost impossible for their congregation to do so. There were a few exceptions, and those were in groups where agreements were reviewed frequently and there was ongoing dialogue on this kind of issue.

If your fellowship is taking a casual approach to audio, your youth will have difficulty surviving our modern times. The pressures they are facing are just too great, the slope too slippery, and it is too easy to purchase music online without accountability. With a single click, any genre of music can be instantly downloaded. While at one time others could see the covers of your albums, which provided some accountability, today it goes directly onto your device and others have no idea what you are listening to. If we are going to use this kind of technology properly, it will require good teaching, continued dialogue, and a strong counterculture stance.

If you are part of a fellowship that is just saying no to audio, there can be some consequences to this approach as well. Your youth may have difficulty with spiritual discernment. We need good teaching regardless of our stance, and this typically doesn't occur in groups that just say no. Another element missing in groups that just say no to audio is fully integrated seekers. For a seeker to successfully integrate into a new culture, there needs to be more than just added restrictions. There should also be new fulfilling and enjoyable opportunities. Changing cultures is difficult and listening to good teaching and worship songs through the week can be helpful in making the change.

A few young people I interviewed said they would be willing to back up on this issue if their leadership asked them to, and it is interesting to note what kind of churches they belonged to. These youth were in groups where music is openly discussed, and a strong relationship is cultivated between the leaders and the youth. The leaders have been able to share a compelling vision, and their youth have embraced that vision and can articulate it.

Creating or Consuming?

In my childhood home, singing was a normal part of growing up. We sang as we drove, my mother sang as she worked, and in the evening we sang as a family after reading from the Bible. Many of us were raised in singing homes, but not every home is this way. We must understand that listening to music is not the same as singing it. In fact, many people openly admit they can't sing. Why not? After all, Americans are consuming more music than ever before.

There is a big difference between creating and consuming. In his book *The Tech-Wise Family*, Andy Crouch laments the fact that secular American families used to know how to sing, but this tradition is being lost. At ballgames, the crowd would sing the National Anthem, but today this has been assigned to the experts. He notes that there was a time when singing together was normal in America:

> Sitting in the living room or on the porch singing together, or listening to one another play instruments, was once a normal part of many American families' lives together. Today, I dare say, for the vast majority of American families it would seem impossibly corny and embarrassing. We can consume more music than

they ever did; we create less music than they ever could have imagined.[1]

There was a time when songs carried a message. Whether it was folk music or songs that retold events, people sang to remember and retain their history. In the not-so-distant past, congregational singing was an expected part of going to church. Then came choirs, keyboards, and worship teams. So much is lost when we lose vibrant congregational singing—we should do whatever it takes to preserve our tradition of song. There are good reasons for recorded audio, and in many ways it is blessing the kingdom of God. But sometimes good becomes the enemy of the best.

Stop for a moment and consider your church. Is your congregational singing increasing in vibrancy? How does the amount of time spent singing as a congregation compare with thirty years ago? Is there more interest in gathering to sing or coming together to listen to a small group perform? It is easy to move from worship to enjoying good performances. We should frequently stop and ask ourselves: Am I consuming more music than I am creating?

PART FIVE

5

RE-EVALUATING OUR COURSE

CHAPTER TWENTY-FIVE

ELECTRONIC SEDUCTION

Raynald peered longingly out the window. Beyond the Castle of Nieuwkerk were green rolling hills, productive fields, and trees lining the beautiful Scheldt River snaking its way through what is known today as Belgium. His mind drifted back to his glorious youthful years. His father had been a wealthy man, a well-known duke. Upon his father's death in 1343, Raynald had succeeded him, inheriting his title and properties. Raynald was only ten years old at the time, and those first years of being a wealthy young duke had been exciting. But all that had changed, and today he found himself imprisoned on one of the very properties he had inherited. The doors were always unlocked, and he had permission to leave whenever he wished, but he stayed in this room for years.

From their youth, Raynald and his younger brother Edward were opposites. Their personalities and interests were different, and they quarreled continuously. The squabbling began when they were very young and continued through their teenage years. Eventually Raynald came of age and took control of the large estates. However, it soon became obvious he lacked the gift of business administration.

Even worse, he lacked self-control. He seemed unable to say no to good food, and eventually the public scorned him for his extreme obesity. The townspeople even nicknamed him Crassus, or The Fat.

The conflict between Raynald and his brother intensified, and after one particularly violent quarrel, Edward led a successful revolt against Raynald, grabbed control of his estates, and took him captive. But he didn't kill his older brother.

Raynald's Room

Instead, Edward built a special room around Raynald in the Nieuwkerk castle. The doors and windows were always open, and Raynald was told he could leave anytime he wished. The only problem was, due to his obesity, he couldn't squeeze out through any of the openings. All he had to do to regain his freedom was lose weight.

Edward knew his older brother's weakness for food, and every day the servants were commanded to surround Raynald with tempting delicacies. Every day brought a fresh smorgasbord of wonderful foods placed temptingly in this room. As his younger brother suspected, Raynald couldn't say no. When the public accused him of cruelty, Edward replied, "My brother is not a prisoner. He may leave whenever he so wills."[1]

History says that Raynald stayed in this room for ten years and wasn't released until Edward was finally killed in battle. By then Raynald's health was so ruined that he died within the year, a prisoner of his own appetite.

I can't help but wonder how many times Raynald decided to reform. How often did he finish a large plate of food and say to himself, "That is the last time I am going to eat that much. I am sick of this, and I have got to lose weight so I can reclaim my life! There are large estates, beautiful homes, and a luxurious life of ease just beyond that door. I have to change my eating habits!" I suspect there were even times when he got angry with his brother and resolved to prove he could control his appetite. But a few hours later, a tempting aroma would waft in from the kitchen, and his resolve would fade. "Just one more meal before I reform!"

An Irresistible Attraction

Our electronic age has many similarities to Raynald's room. Many individuals I interviewed spoke of the difficulty of relinquishing specific uses of technology, even those that could be a spiritual detriment. Like Raynald, they know change is needed, but they have difficulty suppressing their appetite. What is it about electronic technology that makes it so difficult to say no? Why do we continue, all the while confessing that something should change?

FOMO

The acronym FOMO (fear of missing out) was coined in 2004 and made it into the *Oxford Dictionary* in 2013.[2] FOMO is one of the reasons we have difficulty saying no. Most of us have had times of wondering what is being said across the room. We see a lively discussion in progress, suspect it is more exciting than the one we are engaged in, and our curiosity grows. We are fearful we are missing out on something interesting. I suspect this has been happening since the beginning of time. It probably wasn't too long after creation that Adam's children saw him whispering to Eve and wondered what they were saying. They were afraid they were missing out. But historically, our curiosity was restricted by the fact that we were only aware of conversations near us—until electronic technology.

Today, we can be connected to a multitude of conversations occurring simultaneously. Everything from the latest on the Middle East conflict to an ongoing political debate to constant updates on Sally's vacation is at your fingertips. The phone beeps, and regardless of what you are doing, your curiosity is aroused. What is happening?

Did something exciting just occur? Is somebody trying to reach you? Is there an interesting conversation that you should be aware of? We know we should let it go and concentrate on the person talking to us or the task at hand. But we are pulled in by FOMO.

Relief from Reality

A survey taken among 18 to 29-year-old Americans showed that 93 percent use their phones to avoid boredom, and 47 percent admitted to reaching for their phone to avoid interacting with people around them.[3] Like a pill promising relief from pain, young people increasingly reach for technology when life becomes difficult. Whether it is a personality conflict in the workplace, tension at home, or bills piling up and a checkbook that's empty, technology offers temporary relief from reality.

Recently I was sitting toward the back of a large auditorium at a conference. Any time a lecturer spent too much time on a point or got wordy in his delivery, a multitude of small screens would light up in the darkened room. Bored listeners were reaching out for relief. We see this happening all around us. Whether watching a movie, using social media instead of being "present" in a relationship, or listening to music, this generation is increasingly turning to technology for relief.

One young man I interviewed spoke of how his youth group uses technology to overcome the social awkwardness inherent in face-to-face relationships. "When we get together it's always, 'Check out this video!' instead of actually having a conversation." He is embarrassed at how much time they can spend going from one video to another, losing track of time, and later realizing how little was accomplished by being together. Many families have used television like this for years. It is easier to focus on a movie than on building interpersonal relationships. But is this really a healthy way for our youth groups to interact? Do we want to raise a generation who can no longer communicate and build authentic relationships?

Faithful Friend

Walk through any mall, airport, or large public gathering place and observe how people interact with their phones. Whether focusing on it while walking through a crowd or absent-mindedly caressing it while looking around, body language reveals that these little devices have become much more than tools. People are building strong relationships with their devices, yet most of us believe we are exempt.[a] Sometimes it is easier to spot this kind of weakness in others than in our own lives. Columnist Katie Reid described her alarm when she saw her young daughter building strong emotional ties to electronic gadgets:

> I don't want my daughter's closest friend to be a phone. Once I realized that, I had to ask myself: "Do I really want *my* closest friend to be a phone?" Our phones have become intimate parts of our lives. We hold them physically close to us all day long. We gaze at them. And, in turn, they are pretty dependable companions. They help distract us when we're bored; they make us feel good about ourselves; and they get us out of awkward social situations.[4]

The columnist went on to say she has abandoned her smartphone for an old-fashioned flip phone. Regardless of how heavily you use electronic technology, you need to understand the risk of developing relationships with these gadgets. We are increasingly allowing ourselves to be controlled by beeps, buzzes, and rings. Whether you use a phone only for verbal conversation or carry a device capable of incredible computing power, you are at risk. It will take conscious effort to keep these devices in their proper place.

God never intended for us to build relationships with inanimate objects. This is called idolatry. We are emotionally needy creatures. And the more electronic technology can do, the greater our tendency will be to turn to our devices rather than to humans.[b]

---

[a] In his article, "The Most Intimate Relationship in Your Life: Your Smartphone," secular writer Tom Chatfield observed, "Our smartphones are among the most sacred and personal of our possessions, rarely out of sight or mind. For many of us, they are the first thing we touch when we wake in the morning and the last thing we touch when we go to bed at night." —<https://99u.adobe.com/articles/41017/the-most-intimate-relationship-in-your-life-your-smartphone>, accessed on May 23, 2018.

[b] Sherry Turkle, addressing this inner craving for relationship, wrote, "Technology is seductive when what it offers meets our human vulnerabilities. And as it turns out, we are very vulnerable indeed." —*Alone Together*, p. 1.

Clickbait

Humans are susceptible to inanimate relationships due to our inherent struggle with real ones, and marketers intentionally prey on this vulnerability. Pictures, slogans, and jazzy jingles are employed to pull us in. This is known as clickbait. Another new term brought on by the Internet, clickbait is "content whose main purpose is to attract attention and encourage visitors to click on a link to a particular web page."[5] The goal is to attract you to their site and keep you there as long as possible. Marketing competition is tough, and advertisers are going to great lengths to get your attention. Usually clever, often misleading, and purposely distracting, these articles lead you along click by click, preying on your secret longings and desires.

> God never intended for us to build relationships with inanimate objects. This is called idolatry.

It is important that we understand what is happening. This tactic has been extremely successful, and it's rare to find an Internet user who hasn't been sucked in. A user fires up his computer intending to pursue a legitimate goal, only to find himself distracted and wasting a tremendous amount of time because he succumbed to the allure of clickbait. Like Raynald imprisoned in his castle because he can't say no to a continual selection of enticing food, we are held captive as long as we continue clicking.

In the last two chapters we reviewed some of the many snares of modern technology. Electronic gadgetry is the vehicle that delivers the godless messages of pop culture and provides constant distraction. Consequently, it is possible to focus on the many ways Satan is using electronic technology and neglect a vital fact—God is also at work! And the same device that can deliver godless, sinful, and spiritually toxic entertainment can be used by God for His purposes.

CHAPTER TWENTY-SIX

OPPORTUNITY OF OUR DAY

One of the marvels of the Roman Empire was their revolutionary transportation system. Today we give little thought to excellent highways, bridges, and engineered infrastructure, but there was a time when good roads in bad weather were almost nonexistent. The Roman government put an incredible amount of thought and energy into developing a first-class system of roads. Previous roads had allowed water to puddle, creating muddy messes during a storm. But Roman roads were built in layers with a solid foundation. They were also cambered, or raised in the middle, permitting rainwater to run off. With crushed compacted gravel, sand, and neatly arranged paving stones, these roads lasted for hundreds of years, and fragments still exist today.

Over the course of 700 years, Rome built more than 55,000 miles of these stone-paved highways throughout Europe. As Roman legions conquered new areas, highways were built connecting these captured cities to the growing empire. This ensured access and allowed their military to move quickly to suppress uprisings and stomp out rebellion. This expertly engineered road system also became the principal connection for commerce. Good roads made transportation of products possible, and as a result, these roads became the primary arteries facilitating business and trade.

There are many similarities between Roman roads in the time of the early church and the World Wide Web today. Military and communication were the initial impetus behind both, and both ended up being used for so much more.

What Was God Up To?
For thousands of years transportation experienced little change. Communication couldn't travel any faster than people, and without a good road system, moving information to new communities was difficult and slow. Is it a coincidence that this huge Roman road project started a few hundred years before Christ appeared? Was it by chance that this vast system of roads was completed just in time to share the good news of the Gospel? The Roman government's militaristic goal in building these roads was self-centered and nationalistic. Yet God took what was meant for evil and used it for incredible good. These same roads that were intended to serve Rome's global agenda allowed the Gospel to spread throughout the known world in an incredibly short period of time.

What Is God Up To?
No matter what your opinion of high-speed networks, satellite communications, fiber optic capabilities, or the World Wide Web, something huge is occurring before our eyes. This time it isn't stone roads connecting newly conquered cities, but the virtual ability to connect with anyone, at any time, almost anywhere on the globe. Suddenly, ways of reaching out that were totally inconceivable just a few years ago are readily available. It's no wonder that many Christians are amazed and excited! We should be asking what God is doing, and how we should use these opportunities. Let's look at a few doors that electronic technology has opened.

Electronic Storage
Recently I talked with a man who has been active for many years

providing literature inside restricted countries. When he first began this ministry, he packed as many Bibles as possible into suitcases and then tried to get through the border without being caught. Today his task is much different. Bibles and other doctrinal writings to encourage the underground churches can be carried on a tiny storage card. These can easily be taken with him and given to believers with little fear of detection. Several of these first-generation believers own print shops, and after the business activity is over for the day, the store closes and printing for the church begins. Using the data on the cards, these small shops can pump out more literature in one night than could have been transported by suitcase in years. The last I talked to him, he is working with five different shops producing material at night, a tremendous blessing to these oppressed followers of Jesus.

> Just as Roman roads paved the way for the Gospel, electronic technology is taking the message of Jesus into some dark corners of the world.

This ability to use electronic storage and print within restricted countries also greatly reduces costs. With overseas shipping costs eliminated, even poor countries are now receiving literature. In a news report one Christian organization said, "We can get these materials into areas where believers are persecuted and in places where the demand for Scripture far outweighs the supply. Even in impoverished areas, we're placing all of this Christian material into the hands of ordinary people who can't afford to buy even one Bible."[1] Just as Roman roads paved the way for the Gospel and the Gutenberg printing press opened the door for the Reformation, electronic technology is taking the message of Jesus into some dark corners of the world.

Anonymous Audio

Fatima winds her way home from the market. Carrying her purchases, she smiles as she passes acquaintances, nods to an older lady sitting on a bench, and then turns onto her street. From outward appearances, Fatima is just one of many people talking, walking, and enjoying the day. She, like almost all young people in her community, is using earbuds. But something is different about Fatima. She is a new believer in Jesus, and she is listening to the New Testament in Arabic.

In Fatima's Islamic setting, no one would dare have a Bible of paper and ink; the risk is simply too high. With earbuds, no one else knows what she is listening to. People on the street assume she is listening to her favorite music. Fatima's life has been changed by this exposure. Every day she listens for hours, trying to learn as much as possible.

Ahmad lives in another Islamic country and has the New Testament on his phone. He loves to sit in the local park and listen, but he has taken this one step further. He shares the Bible electronically with anyone who will take it. Evangelism is extremely risky, but after much fervent prayer, Ahmed has transferred copies of his audio Bible to several friends. Ahmad's family is not aware that he has embraced Christianity, and he prays often for direction. How will he be able to share with them what has happened in his life?

In restricted countries, similar scenarios occur every day. Small MP3 players prerecorded with the Bible in the native tongue are being distributed in some dark places. Several years ago, I talked to a believer by phone who was working in a very restricted area. People were coming to faith through visions, and they were asking for audio Bibles. That very day, another seeking soul had come to the Lord. "I feel so helpless," the worker told me. "This person has confessed faith in Jesus, but I have no way to disciple these new believers. I can't be in their area, so all I can do is give them one of these audio Bibles." A few weeks later this missionary called again. "I don't know why I was so concerned. The new believers I told you about have been listening to that Bible for the last few weeks and are coming to the right conclusion regarding holiness of life. The

Holy Spirit is at work! I don't know why I thought I needed to be involved!" Similar scenarios play out around the globe daily, and God is using technology in some astonishing ways.

Wireless Witness

Hannah remembers huddling with her father next to an illegal radio in the closed country of North Korea. Her father had managed to obtain a radio, and Hannah first heard the Gospel message while listening to South Korean broadcasting in secret. Years later, Hannah escaped to South Korea. Her family was planning to join her later, but security tightened, and she has never seen them since.

Her knowledge of Christianity was very limited, but one night Hannah decided to enter a South Korean church. Eventually she was converted, professed faith in Jesus, and became a member of this little church. Hannah continued to grow in faith and made a life for herself in South Korea. But she longed for a way to reach out to the many, including her family, still held captive by North Korea. Her church leader told her of a Christian radio station that broadcasted into North Korea and needed help. Hannah thought of those nights as a child secretly listening to the radio with her father, and she knew what she should do. Today she works in a studio, broadcasting in her North Korean dialect and trying to reach out with the Bible to those across the border. While she may not see the results of her labors in this life, she is confident that people are listening.[2]

While much broadcasting opposes Christianity, there are places where the radio waves are being put to good use. This occurs not only in restricted countries like North Korea, but also in very poor countries and places that still do not have Bibles translated into their mother tongue. Radio broadcasts and inexpensive transistor radios that only receive the channel providing Christian teaching are a powerful way to reach these dark places.

Website Witness

Roughly one quarter of the world's population believes that

Muhammad was a messenger of Allah, and the Islamic religion continues to grow rapidly. While global population is projected to grow more than 30 percent in the coming decades, the Islamic faith is expected to increase by 70 percent, more than twice as fast as the world population. Yet despite this rapid growth there are an increasing number of seekers within this huge Muslim population. Some are having dreams, others have become disillusioned with Islam after being persecuted by fellow Muslims, and still others are simply curious about Christianity. But many of these seekers have a problem. Asking questions or seeking information about other religions can be dangerous. Because of this, millions of Muslim seekers are turning to the Internet.

In the privacy of their homes, without even their family being aware, Muslims can use their computers or phones to investigate Christianity. A Christian organization that operates a website specifically for Muslim seekers recently reported an average of over 5 million interactions with seekers on Facebook each month. And this is just one organization! The same anonymity that allows men to secretly access Internet pornography also allows seekers to safely encounter the Gospel. For millions today, this is their only access to truth.

I read of a believer in Saudi Arabia. His initial exposure to the Gospel was through an online discipleship course, but eventually he made contact in another country. He traveled there for a week of teaching, professed Jesus, was baptized, and returned to Saudi Arabia. Even though there are an estimated 1.4 million believers scattered throughout the country, this young man doesn't know any of them. Today he continues to receive spiritual support online.[3]

Many more isolated seekers are finding answers to their spiritual questions online. Some of them live in areas where physical persecution is intense. A prime example is Iran. While getting exact numbers of Christians is difficult, in 1979 there were an estimated 360 believers in the entire country. That number has grown to an estimated 360,000,[4] and their religious leaders are quite alarmed. One of their ayatollahs (Muslim religious leaders) recently condemned Iranian government officials "for their negligence in preparing counteracting strategies to stop the spread of Christianity."[5] It is difficult to keep seekers from accessing Christian material in the privacy of their own homes.

In 2014 David Garrison wrote the book *A Wind in the House of Islam*, documenting the recent surge in conversions of Muslims to Christianity. For centuries Christian missionaries have tried to reach out to followers of Muhammed with little success. Yet recently God is moving among these people in unprecedented ways. In the first chapter Garrison says:

> Something is happening today that is challenging the hold that Islam exercises over its adherents. Muslim movements to Jesus Christ are taking place in numbers we've never seen before. For the sake of clarity and consistency, let's define a movement of Muslims to Christ to be at least 100 new church starts or 1,000 baptisms that occur over a two-decade period. Today, in more than 70 separate locations in 29 nations, new movements of Muslim followers of Christ are taking place . . . In some countries the numbers within these new movements have grown to tens of thousands.[6]

God is at work among these people, and electronic technology is one of the tools His children are using to reach out.

Amazing Opportunity

Imagine a Jewish man in Palestine just before the time of Christ. After years of being dominated by a cruel regime, he is ready for change. He is tired of watching the expansion of the oppressive Roman Empire. When will the promised Messiah come and free Israel from this tyranny? Everywhere he looks, Rome's power and evil influence permeate his land and culture. He steps outside his house, only to find Roman engineers marking out yet another highway. When will this ever end? Frustration wells up as he watches. Rome's organized methods, excellent planning, and state-of-the-art engineering are marvelous, yet disturbing. Rome is growing more powerful by the day!

I suspect many Jewish men struggled with these conflicting emotions as they watched the Roman road-building explosion. I wonder if their thoughts were similar to mine as I watch electronic expansion. I see yet another fiber optic cable being buried in my neighborhood or read of a new satellite being launched into space and feel disheartened. My mind goes to the masses bowing down to the god of entertainment, the millions polluting their minds each day with pornography, and the growing spread of evil around the globe.

But is it possible I am forgetting that God is at work as well?

CHAPTER TWENTY-SEVEN

HOW SHOULD CHURCHES PREPARE?

It was 8:30 in the morning, December 26, 2004. Ten-year-old Tilly Smith walked onto Maikhao Beach with her family and experienced a strange sensation. Something about the scene brought back memories she couldn't immediately identify. Suddenly she knew what it was.

Tilly, a British schoolgirl on winter vacation with her parents in Thailand, had been sitting in class just two weeks before.

> Normally I was bored during geography, but our teacher, Andrew Kearney, had shown us a video of a tsunami in Hawaii, and it had been really gripping. As we walked toward the beach, I started to have a really weird feeling. The sea was high on the sand, and I noticed waves were coming in but not going out. The sea was 'fizzing,' and there was froth on the waves. I kept thinking, *I've seen this, I've seen this somewhere.* I felt something terrible was going to happen.

She was just a young girl, hardly the person you would expect to sound an alarm. But as the water began to retreat, she couldn't keep quiet. "All the things I was seeing had been in the video we'd seen in geography. They were signs a tsunami was about to hit, and soon!"[1]

At the time few people in the Western world, including Tilly's parents, had ever heard the word *tsunami*. So when Tilly started shouting "Tsunami! There's going to be a tsunami!" people on Maikhao Beach didn't know what she was talking about. As Tilly continued to run back and forth, shouting at people and telling them to get off the beach, the urgency in her voice caused them to respond. Just minutes after her family found refuge on the third floor of their hotel, the tsunami hit.[2] Over two hundred thousand people lost their lives that day, five thousand from Thailand alone. But thanks to the cry of a ten-year-old girl, no one on Maikhao Beach was killed.

There were times, after a day of listening to Anabaptists tell about their experiences with technology, when I felt a little like Tilly Smith. A young man would share his ongoing struggle with pornography, lamenting that people in his church don't seem very concerned. Then a church leader (sometimes from the same congregation) would walk in and calmly say he thought things were going well. One leader seemed confident because he had rules in place, and another seemed pleased that he didn't; but both displayed a strange lack of urgency. Most Anabaptist church constituencies that I interviewed have members who are struggling. So what should churches be doing?

How Should We View Technology?
Earlier we looked at the deterministic view (technology itself possesses an intrinsic power and desire to dominate) and the instrumental view (technology is just a servant of the user). This issue continues to be debated in secular circles, but how should the follower of Jesus regard this question? Is there something intrinsically evil within electronic technology, or is technology amoral—good or evil based on our usage? My interviews indicated that most of us believe the latter. A computer isn't evil or good inherently. Yet, if it is neutral, why do we continue to struggle? Why does this issue fester in many of our churches?

I propose that there are many similarities between electronic technology and money.

Money: Is It Good or Bad?

How would you answer that question? We can think of times when money has been a tremendous blessing and its use a wonderful testimony. We know that finances also can be a tremendous snare. Yet most of us prefer to believe that money is neutral. We like to think it has no moral inclination of itself and that its goodness, or lack thereof, is determined solely by the heart of the user.

But if money is neutral, why didn't the New Testament writers just address the heart and its selfish desires? The teachings of Jesus and His followers focus heavily on the dangers of wealth itself.[a] In fact, if you use the New Testament to determine how much money you should have, you won't find much encouragement to accumulate a large savings account. Jesus even said that a rich man will have great difficulty entering the kingdom of heaven.[b] But if money has no power of its own, why all the concern? I believe the answer is simple. Wealth brings strong temptation to even the godliest saint. Few, if any, can completely avoid its enticement.

If we could just decide that money is wrong, then dealing with it would be easy. We can't do that, however, so we must wrestle with how to use it without being overcome. Although the Bible does not teach that money is wrong, its many warnings show us the need for constant Holy Spirit discernment as we use it.

The same is true of electronic technology. It would be much simpler if we could just decide that all gadgets, from calculators and alarm clocks to computers and phones, are wrong and should be avoided. But that is not realistic, and churches will continue to face a myriad of difficult decisions. So how should churches prepare for the coming tsunami? As the waters continue to rise and the waves

---

[a] Matthew 13:22; 1 Timothy 6:9–11
[b] Matthew 19:23

get higher, there are a few essential elements to consider: better methods, the importance of defense, and a vision beyond ourselves.

Churches must search for better methods. It is extremely difficult to change group culture and long-standing traditions. But we need to recognize that traditional methods of dealing with threats to church community may not be enough to protect us against this encroaching danger. If an old technique isn't working, let's admit it and prayerfully look for answers. We will need more honest transparency in our church relationships, and this is especially difficult for older, more traditional churches.

Earlier we looked at two approaches that are obviously not working. One is to keep using rules without good teaching or relationships, and the other is to relegate the issue to parents and let them deal with it. Ironically, these two approaches, practiced by churches with opposite views on outward conservatism, have something in common. Both are trying to find a safe, easy, risk-free road.

God intends His kingdom to be more powerful than culture. A church able to face current and future challenges needs a clear Biblical vision and open dialogue, collectively addressing each threat and its hidden influence. This requires leaders who are willing to take risks, address difficult topics, and speak out on issues that touch hidden areas of our lives. This also requires a higher level of personal accountability than many churches have thought necessary.

The churches faring the best are intentional in this area. Some have assigned each person an accountability partner. These partners meet regularly and ask each other difficult questions about daily devotional life, online activity, and purity of thought life. They can share struggles and pray for specific areas of personal weakness. Other churches employ small accountability groups that meet regularly.

Maybe all of this sounds a little scary, but the cry from our young people should not be ignored! They are facing temptations unknown to previous generations. The battle is fierce, and daily enticements threaten to derail their spiritual lives. The enemy's tactics have changed, and his weapons are stronger. God is still able to deliver, but it is foolish to assume we can withstand amplified spiritual warfare without increased spiritual vigilance.

> It is foolish to assume we can withstand amplified spiritual warfare without increased spiritual vigilance.

While Internet filters can be a great blessing and a powerful tool in this battle, they will never replace the growing need for personal accountability. Churches that are going to survive the onslaught of electronic technology will need to make changes to counteract it.

Churches must understand the importance of defense. Earlier we looked at the military teaching "defense is the strongest form of combat in which you always lose" and how it applies to churches. Our churches must do more than just say no to the newest technology. But defense is still vital—trying to wage war while neglecting defensive measures is a formula for failure.

Community is extremely important, and we dare not minimize its significance as we face social pressure. To assume that young people can fight against a strong cultural current with only periodic bursts of theological teaching is wishful thinking. Sound teaching is essential, but we also need strong church communities that band together against the enemy.[c] God has a reason for placing us into biological families, and converts to Christ are birthed into church families for the same reason. We need protection and support!

We shouldn't be afraid of brotherhood agreements regarding

---

[c] Protestant theologian and sociologist Peter Berger said, "Unless our theologian has the inner fortitude of a desert saint, he has only one effective remedy against the threat of cognitive collapse in the face of these pressures. He must huddle together with like-minded fellow deviants—and huddle very closely. Only in a counter community of considerable strength does cognitive deviance have a chance to maintain itself. This counter community provides continuing therapy against the creeping doubt as to whether after all one may not be wrong and the majority right." —Peter Berger, *A Rumor of Angels*, Anchor Books, Garden City, New York, 1969, p. 17.

electronic technology, but neither should we assume that rules alone will resolve the issue. Anabaptist speaker and writer Matt Landis puts it like this: "A written rule must be derived from vigorous congregational thought, discussion, and deliberation . . . the important thing being congregational involvement, and the written rule being an artifact of the group's communal life and desire."[3] At times leaders must make decisions, even though they may not meet the mindset of every member. But if pursuing Jesus instead of surrounding culture is not part of a church's DNA, then adding rules is meaningless.

Technology is changing rapidly. To collectively make decisions, we need to revisit these agreements on a regular basis to ensure they are helping us reach our goals.

Churches must have a vision beyond themselves. To survive this tsunami, we need the blessing of God. The enemy is coming in like a flood, and we need spiritual wisdom and direction. If a church is no longer concerned about the things that concern God, just how much protection will He give? It is easy to analyze every question solely by how it will affect our church, our reputation, or our image. Jesus described His mission in these words: "For the Son of man is come to seek and to save that which was lost."[d] If our churches are going to view technology correctly, we need God's presence and power in our midst. And if we expect Him to empower our churches, our mission needs to agree with His.

Having concern for others and a forward vision is critical to healthy church life. It's somewhat like riding a bicycle. One could assume that the easiest way to avoid falling over is to focus on staying upright. However, the best way to stay upright on a bicycle is to be going somewhere. Forward motion keeps a bike from falling over. Our churches are the same.

At one time most members of Anabaptist churches were involved in farming or other agriculturally based occupations. Now we are

---

[d] Luke 19:10

increasingly pushed into trades and businesses that require increased use of technology. Sometimes we fight this shift; it seems uncomfortable. Life seemed better back on the farm. God's eye, however, is still on redeeming this lost and broken world, and if we seize the moment, the push into the business world can provide tremendous opportunity. Sharing our faith with coworkers and other business associates has a purifying effect on our own lives. Those we are trying to reach are adept at pointing out hypocrisy and inconsistencies. We desperately need their observations!

One of the best defenses against the tech tsunami is a church that walks close to God. A church that embraces His vision of reaching out to the lost. A church that actively and prayerfully pursues a strong defensive—and offensive—strategy. Such a church has God's blessing and is better prepared to face the challenges.

This isn't a time to fear the future or to unduly stress over coming changes. Peter said God has "given unto us all things that pertain unto life and godliness,"[e] and that promise still stands. That doesn't mean the future will be easy. Our churches cannot survive with a "business as usual" mentality while resting on our laurels. We need young men with clear vision, old men willing to dream,[f] and congregations prayerfully working together and focusing on God's objectives. As we do this, God will be with us.

---

[e] 2 Peter 1:3
[f] Joel 2:28; Acts 2:17

CHAPTER TWENTY-EIGHT

HIGHER GROUND

Walking along the beach at Banda Aceh, Indonesia, it was difficult to visualize the tragedy. The sun sparkled off the surf, gulls circled and called out, and water gently lapped the shore. I tried to imagine what it would be like to suddenly see a gigantic wave rushing toward me. Nine years after the terrible tsunami, the cliff high above me still had grooves left by the one-hundred-foot wall of water that came crashing inland.

What is the proper response when a tsunami is heading your way? As I stood on that beach at Banda Aceh, it was clear there were not many options. You can't stop a tsunami, and you aren't going to outrun one. It's too late to build a structure, and even if you could, few buildings can withstand the violent force, as the remains of many structures testified. There is only one thing to do.

If you are going to survive a tsunami, you must seek higher ground.

None of us can fathom the strength of this tech tsunami or all the ways it will affect our lives and churches. Changes are already happening rapidly in robotics, artificial intelligence, genetic engineering, and virtual reality. These changes will undoubtedly raise challenges and ethical questions we can't foresee. The water is churning, and we know what is coming will affect every aspect of our lives. So what are we to do?

Seeking Higher Ground

Our churches must be awake, aware, and actively addressing this issue. But we cannot stop there. Not everyone is blessed to be part of a fellowship that is seriously confronting this problem. Therefore it is essential that we prepare *personally* for the coming onslaught. Regardless how often your congregation meets (and it should be often), or how much dialogue you have (and there should be plenty), or how much thought you give to collective agreements (and that should be much), ultimately it will be your personal connection with God that will empower you to survive and thrive in this tech tsunami.

We are invariably drawn to technology because it promises what we naturally long for—ease and efficiency. We are naturally impatient and constantly looking for anything to accomplish our goals faster. Ironically, the more efficient we become, the higher our expectations and the greater our propensity for disappointment. Higher efficiency seldom translates into greater contentment. Yet shunning all technology doesn't seem to be the answer either. God intends that we think, create, and improve. Failing to do this is failing to live in His image.

Before you rejoice, hug yourself, and go back to your electronic gadgetry, please understand this: to reach higher ground as the tsunami approaches, you need to prayerfully consider whether your technology helps your walk with God. Hold it loosely, aware that God may call you to abandon something that initially had advantages. As we learned from the interviews, this isn't easy. As things continue to change rapidly, you desperately need the spiritual discernment to decide what technology to employ, what to abandon, and how to properly utilize what you keep.

To effectively develop this spiritual discernment, I believe we need to grow in some crucial disciplines.

Essential Spiritual Disciplines

Disciplines and spiritual rituals[a] are not popular in much of modern Christianity, but men of God have used them throughout history. The writer of Psalm 119 writes, "Seven times a day do I praise thee because of thy righteous judgments,"[b] and David commits to praying in the "evening, and morning, and at noon."[c] We see men like Daniel, so consistent and disciplined in prayer that his enemies knew exactly at which window and what time he would kneel there. Throughout the Old Testament God used regular festivals, feasts, and other special events to help His people remember Him. We also see this in the early church. In the Acts of the Apostles, Luke mentions the "hour of prayer, being the ninth hour."[d] Apparently that was the customary time of day to gather for prayer.

In our day, rituals and disciplines have fallen out of favor. Doing the same thing over and over tends to be seen as lifeless and worthless. But notice Paul's warning to Timothy that the "latter times" would be difficult, and many people would "depart from the faith."[e] Then he gave Timothy a list of things to do and concluded by saying, "Take heed unto thyself, and unto the doctrine; continue in them: for in doing this thou shalt both save thyself, and them that hear thee."[f]

Notice the phrase "continue in them." These words speak of doing the same thing over and over in preparation for coming challenges. Paul was calling Timothy to some very basic, vital spiritual rituals, or Christian training exercises. He was encouraging Timothy to keep seeking higher ground! Paul also told Timothy, "Exercise thyself rather unto godliness."[g] It would be wise for us to go back and examine some

---

[a] *Ritual,* as we are using it here, is a "religious action or behavior that is performed regularly." While rituals have no inherent power of themselves, they provide essential structure in daily life. Spiritual rituals can also help us step out of the daily scurry and allow us to focus on the glory of God Himself. The result? We can be slowly changed into His image (2 Corinthians 3:18).

[b] Psalm 119:164

[c] Psalm 55:17

[d] Acts 3:1

[e] 1 Timothy 4:1

[f] 1 Timothy 4:16

[g] 1 Timothy 4:7

of these essential Christian disciplines found in Scripture.

Prayer and Fasting

Fervent prayer is crucial to developing healthy spiritual discernment. I challenge you to analyze your daily prayer life. Is your connection with God vibrant enough to take you through what is coming? Are you close enough to God to hear what He is saying? Does "praying always with all prayer and supplication in the Spirit, and watching thereunto with all perseverance and supplication"[h] describe your prayer life?

And what about fasting? Jesus told His followers how to survive after He returned to heaven. "But the days will come, when the bridegroom shall be taken away from them, and then shall they fast in those days."[i] Is fasting a part of your spiritual life? I sense we are living in "those days," a time when we need to fast more, yet we are doing it less. Fasting is a discipline that helps keep our fleshly appetites in subjection. If you are serious about surviving the coming challenges, I suggest you integrate regular prayer and fasting into your life.

Reading and Meditation

"Till I come, give attendance to reading."[j] This passage may refer to the public reading of Scripture, but it can also apply to personal reading. Paul knew Timothy would need to diligently read the Word of God and give heed to it if he was going to survive. He was not speaking about just reading a brief devotional or a few verses each morning, but of taking time to absorb God's message. "Meditate upon these things: give thyself wholly to them."[k]

When steeping a cup of tea, we don't drop the tea bag in and then yank it out. We give the water time to extract the flavor. The same applies as you study God's Word. Take time to meditate on what God is saying. How do the principles of the passage pertain to your current

---

[h] Ephesians 6:18
[i] Luke 5:35
[j] 1 Timothy 4:13
[k] 1 Timothy 4:15

decisions? As you make technological choices, you want the principles of God's Word to guide you. Meditation lets the Word sink deep and come alive, giving the Spirit an opportunity to reveal crucial principles. Aim to integrate this essential discipline into your daily life.

Praise and Worship

Praise is joyfully thanking God for His goodness and for all He has done. David said, "Every day will I bless thee; and I will praise thy name for ever and ever."[1] Verbally praising God should be part of every day. Worship goes further, however. It goes deeper and is directly connected with our values. Worship realigns our priorities and keeps first things first. True worship will always bring about praise, but we can verbally praise God without worshiping Him.

Why is this so important within the context of technology? Electronic technology will keep changing and accomplishing more incredible things than we can imagine. Consequently, our culture will become even more enthralled. People will increasingly see technology as the answer to society's ills, and we will be tempted to do the same. If we are going to use the blessing of technology without worshiping it (ascribing undue value to it), we need to strengthen this vital discipline of praising and worshiping God. "We must watch for signs that our worship is veering off course," one author has warned. "We can no longer simply worship God in admiration or pray to Him without a compulsive fidgeting for our phones. We talk more about God than to Him."[1]

No matter how amazing technology becomes, it must not become more important to us than a tool designed to assist. While electronic technology can do great things, it becomes useless when disconnected from its power source. God alone is life giving, life sustaining, and worthy of our praise and worship. A.W. Tozer, years before the electronic wave, was concerned about the influence that modernism was having on people's pursuit of God. "We have lost our spirit of

---

[1] Psalm 145:2

worship and our ability to withdraw inwardly to meet God in adoring silence,"[2] he lamented. As the intensity and clamor of gadgetry increases, we need to keep reminding ourselves of this. Purposely praise the Lord aloud each day, sing hymns of praise together as a family, and set aside specific times to worship privately. These Christian disciplines are vital to maintaining our focus on God.

Silence and Solitude

Jesus at times sought solitude in the busyness and pressure of life. Immediately after hearing that His cousin John had been beheaded, Jesus "departed . . . into a desert place apart."[m] Mark says that Jesus told His disciples, "Come ye yourselves apart into a desert place, and rest awhile: for there were many coming and going, and they had no leisure so much as to eat."[n] Though Jesus had perfect communion with His Father, He found it necessary to carve out specific times for silence and solitude to separate Himself from the disappointments, stress, and continual chaos of daily life.

If Jesus felt this need two thousand years ago in the relative serenity of Galilee, I wonder how He would respond to our beeping, buzzing, vibrating world. Throughout Scripture, men like Moses, Elijah, and the Apostle Paul, who were used by God in mighty ways, spent time alone in the desert. While God may not give everyone the luxury of physically withdrawing from society, spiritual survival requires that we pursue periodic times of silence and solitude. Donald Whitney makes this observation: "One of the costs of technological advancement is a greater temptation to avoid quietness. While we have broadened our intake of news and information of all kinds, these advantages may come at the expense of our spiritual depth if we do not practice silence and solitude."[3]

Getting Above the Fray

Jesus was passing through Jericho, and Zacchaeus desperately desired

---

[m] Matthew 14:13
[n] Mark 6:31

to see this man the crowd kept talking about. But Zacchaeus was short, and the crowd was pressing in. So he did something unusual for wealthy men in his day. Zacchaeus ran ahead of the crowd and climbed a sycamore tree.º His desire drove him to measures that probably seemed culturally offbeat, but enabled him to climb above the fray for a clearer view of Jesus. If we are going to survive in this constant electronic clamor and information overload, we need to do the same.ᵖ

Jesus encouraged His followers to be serious about personal holiness. He said if your right eye is causing you to stumble, you should "pluck it out, and cast it from thee: for it is profitable to thee that one of thy members should perish, and not that thy whole body should be cast into hell."ᵠ I suggest that we will need to carefully scrutinize which technologies to embrace and which to cast from us. To live "without rebuke in the midst of a crooked and perverse nation,"ʳ we need to take our technological choices very seriously. Let's look at a few ways we can rise above the fray.

Limit your connectivity. We may need a little "technological skepticism," a healthy reluctance to immediately embrace every advancement. Some innovations do tasks quicker but not better, and some that do the job better may not be worth the cost to your family and spiritual wellbeing. This is not a Luddite rejection of all technology. Rather, it involves cautiously and prayerfully analyzing each specific technology as it comes. Even if the new device does the job better, how will it impact your relationships with your family, the people around you, and ultimately with God?

Develop healthy rhythms of engagement and withdrawal. There were times when Jesus actively taught, preached, healed, and challenged His followers. Masses thronged Him, and at one point

---

º Luke 19:4
ᵖ Flannery O'Connor said, "Push back against the age as hard as it pushes against you." —*The Habit of Being: The Letters of Flannery O'Connor,* First Farrar, Straus, Giroux, New York, 1979, p. 229.
ᵠ Matthew 5:29
ʳ Philippines 2:15

the press was so strong that seekers tore off a roof to gain access.[5] Jesus was thoroughly engaged in His work, but He also had times when He purposely withdrew into the desert.

This rhythm of engagement and withdrawal needs to be part of your life fabric as well. The concept of the Sabbath confirms this. God wanted His people to periodically cease their hurried activities, as good as those activities were. So it is with technology. You need to make technological fasts a priority—times of turning off phones and other devices and coming apart for a time.

We have difficulty with balance. We either want to be constantly engaged or continually in a state of withdrawal from the needs around us. Don't allow yourself to be pulled into either error. God intends that we work together with Him as stewards of what He has given us. Yet we are also finite and weak. If we are going to be effective, we must develop healthy rhythms of engagement and withdrawal.

Purpose to be present. We are becoming a nation of multitaskers, and technology is encouraging us along this road. Multitasking sounds wonderfully efficient. Yet I find that I am not as good at accomplishing several tasks at once as I had imagined. Our culture is increasingly driven by time. While this creates a very industrious culture, the offshoot is that those who pursue production tend to neglect personal relationships. We have become a nation of overachievers. We form attachments to devices that increase efficiency, and then we don't take time for the interpersonal relationships that really matter.

Just travel to developing countries and you will soon be asking whose priorities are superior. As one African man told a European reporter. "In Europe you have watches, but in Africa we have time!"[4] Texting while talking to others, or trying to keep up on social media when the family

> In Europe you have watches, but in Africa we have time!

---

[5] Mark 2:4

is together may seem efficient. But it can weaken and even destroy something of greater value. If we want to strengthen and build healthy relationships that matter, we will need to be physically and mentally present. Each device has an off button—learn to use it!

> Each device has an off button—learn to use it!

Teach your children to "swim." There are places on the globe where water is scarce and knowing how to swim is unimportant. There are other places where water is everywhere. I once visited a Cambodian home that was built on stilts. To get there, we had to use a boat. In fact, the entire village was on stilts, and the stores were on small boats that floated from house to house. If you lived there, swimming would be one of the first things your child should learn. The importance of learning to swim is in direct proportion to the amount of surrounding water.

In the past, technology was off in the distance, something we could just stay away from. But those days are over. We are surrounded by it, and as the water continues to rise in our culture, teaching our children to "swim" is no longer optional—it is crucial. We are not able to completely avoid this tech tsunami, and our children must understand how to navigate the coming challenges. This doesn't mean they need constant exposure. But it does mean they need to know Biblical principles that apply to each innovation. Show them by example how to pray before accepting something new. Demonstrate spiritual disciplines in your daily life. We can no longer retreat and hope the water goes away. It isn't going to.

Remember, you don't need to know everything. We are naturally curious. We want to know what is happening and have that inherent FOMO—fear of missing out. Electronic technology can deliver much more information than we are humanly capable of processing. If we are going to thrive in this onslaught of information, we must sort and restrict what comes in. There are three basic categories of information available today via electronic technology:

The Destructive. Information in this category is deadly to our spiritual lives. It includes pornography, Hollywood productions, and a host of other materials that are detrimental to followers of Jesus.

The Essential. This is useful information that helps us do our jobs and live productive lives. It includes research, education, and many other electronic resources that are beneficial and contribute to our well-being. This is the platform our world is using to communicate, and there are many excellent ways we can use technology to connect with the hurting, the disillusioned, and the lost.

The Nonessential. This is information that is not explicitly destructive, yet for many, it poses a greater danger to spiritual life than the other two. It fills our lives with clamor, clutter, and constant commotion. If we are not extremely vigilant, continual beeps, buzzes, and vibrations keep us connected with occurrences around the globe, yet disconnected from God and close relationships. We were not made to know everything all the time. We must restrict the amount of nonessential information we access.

Huge changes have already taken place, and more are coming. Every church and follower of Jesus must ask an important question: How do we maintain a Biblical, Christ-centered worldview while rapidly moving into a post-modern (and increasingly post-truth) environment? We should be holding this up before the Lord. Incredible challenges are coming, and sometimes we wish God would speak more distinctly into our daily decisions. At times the prospect of constant change fills our hearts with fear, and we tend to retreat into a mental cocoon. Just surviving spiritual disaster is our primary goal, and visualizing anything greater is difficult.

God is still in control, and you have been placed in this world by His design. Rest assured that nothing occurring today is outside of His knowledge and control. It is no accident that you are alive at a time when the very mores of society seem to be coming unglued. It isn't by cosmic chance that you and your congregation are living in a world that seems to be spinning out of control. As Mordecai told Esther many years ago, "Who knoweth whether thou art come into the kingdom for such a time as this?"[t]

I challenge you to aim higher than mere survival. God is at work in our world and has promised to be with us. He has assured us that He will never leave us,[u] told us that His power is greater than all the powers of darkness,[v] and promised that He will never allow temptations to come that are greater than we can bear.[w] God is able and willing to protect us against whatever might come.

So seek higher ground and actively engage in kingdom warfare. God's goal is larger than having people sit safely under His protection, pursuing risk-free lives. God is looking for individuals and congregations who are willing to join Him in the battle. His desire is that you labor together with Him[x] to build and nurture His kingdom. Electronic technology isn't taking our God by surprise, and His goal in the coming years is not that we merely survive, but that we thrive!

---

[t] Esther 4:14
[u] Hebrew 13:5
[v] 1 John 4:4
[w] 1 Corinthians 10:13
[x] 1 Corinthians 3:9

ENDNOTES

CHAPTER 1

[1] Intel Corporation, "50 Years of Moore's Law," [video clip], <http://www.intel.com/content/www/us/en/silicon-innovations/moores-law-technology.html>, accessed on 5/23/17.

[2] Wikisource, "Encyclopedia Britannica," <https://en.wikisource.org/wiki/Encyclop%C3%A6dia_Britannica>, accessed on 5/18/17.

CHAPTER 2

[1] Conrad Gessner, *The Bibliotheca Univeralis,* Zurich, 1545.

[2] Nicholas Jolley, ed., *The Cambridge Companion to Leibniz,* Cambridge University Press, United Kingdom, 1995, p. 61.

[3] David Crowley and Paul Heyer, *Communication in History,* Routledge Publishers, London, 2016, p. 84.

[4] *The Sanitarian,* Vol. XL, New York, January 4, 1883, p. 258.

[5] Gary Marshal, "12 Technologies That Scared the World Senseless," Techradar, May 18, 2014, <http://www.techradar.com/news/world-of-tech/12-technologies-that-scared-the-world-senseless-1249053>, accessed on 5/18/17.

[6] George W. Melville, "The Engineer and the Problem of Aerial Navigation," *North American Review,* December, 1901, p. 830.

[7] Carolyn Marvin, *When Old Technologies Were New,* Oxford University Press, New York, 1988, p. 68.

[8] Richard Conniff, "What the Luddites Really Fought Against," *Smithsonian Magazine,* March, 2011.

[9] CNN, "Emails 'Hurt People More Than Pot' " <http://edition.cnn.com/2005/WORLD/europe/04/22/text.iq/?_sm_au_=iHVmJ6q6HC3r5L63>, accessed on 5/19/17.

[10] Daily Mail, "How Using Facebook Could Raise Your Risk of Cancer," February 19, 2009, <http://www.dailymail.co.uk/health/article-1149207/How-using-Facebook-raise-risk-cancer.html>, accessed on 5/19/17.

[11] Science News, "Twitter and Facebook Could Harm Moral Values, Scientists Warn," April 13, 2009, <http://www.telegraph.co.uk/news/science/science-news/5149195/Twitter-and-Facebook-could-harm-moral-values-scientists-warn.html>, accessed on 5/19/17.

[12] Nicholas Carr, "Is Google Making Us Stupid?" *The Atlantic,* July/August 2008.

CHAPTER 3

[1] Your Dictionary, <http://www.yourdictionary.com/technology>, accessed on 5/19/17.

[2] Jason Tanz, "Soon We Won't Program Computers. We'll Train Them Like Dogs," *Wired,* May 2016, <https://www.wired.com/2016/05/the-end-of-code/>, accessed on 5/23/17.

[3] Andreas von Bubnoff, "Robots Master Reproduction," *Nature,* May 11, 2005, <http://www.nature.com/news/2005/050509/full/news050509-6.html>, accessed on 5/23/17.

[4] Abinaya Vijayaraghavan, "Elon Musk on Mission to Link Human Brains with Computers in Four Years: Report," *Reuters,* April 21, 2017, <https://ca.reuters.com/article/businessNews/idCAKBN17N0CU-OCABS>, accessed on 3/23/18.

[5] Tom Goodwin, "The Battle Is for the Customer Interface," *TechCrunch,* March 3, 2015 <https://techcrunch.com/2015/03/03/in-the-age-of-disintermediation-the-battle-is-all-for-the-customer-interface/>, accessed on 4/8/18.

CHAPTER 4

[1] Martin Chalakoski, "Aircraft Inventor Santos-Dumont Believed Air Travel Would Bring World Peace So He Offered His Designs Free of Charge," *The Vintage News,* July 10, 2017, <https://www.thevintagenews.com/2017/07/10/%D0%B0ircraft-inventor-santos-dumont-believed-air-travel-would-bring-world-peace-so-he-offered-his-designs-free-of-charge/>, accessed on 12/30/18.

[2] Association for Safe International Road Travel, "Road Safety Facts," <https://www.asirt.org/safe-travel/road-safety-facts/>, accessed on 2/12/19.

[3] Richard Rhodes, *Visions of Technology,* Simon & Schuster, New York, 1999, p. 308.

[4] Michael J. Coren, "Musk and Zuckerberg Are Fighting Over Whether We Rule Technology—Or It Rules Us," *Quartz,* April 1, 2018, <https://qz.com/1242331/musk-and-zuckerberg-are-fighting-over-whether-we-rule-technology-or-it-rules-us/>, accessed on 4/4/18.

[5] Michael Schmidt, ed., *The Harvill Book of Poetry,* The Harvil Press, London, 1999, p. 553.

[6] Wendell Berry, *The Gift of the Good Land,* North Point Press, San Francisco, 1982, p. 180.

CHAPTER 5

[1] *The Washington Post,* "The Unabomber Trial: The Manifesto,"<http://www.washingtonpost.com/wp-srv/national/longterm/unabomber/manifesto.text.htm>, accessed on 6/26/17.

[2] Nicholas Carr, *The Shallows: What the Internet Is Doing to Our Brains,* W.W Norton and Company, New York, 2011, p. 46.

[3] Marshall McLuhan, *Understanding Media,* The MIT Press, Cambridge, Massachusetts, 1964, p. 11.

[4] Kevin Kelly, *What Technology Wants,* Penguin Books, New York, 2010, p. 171.

[5] Ibid., p. 351.

[6] Dietrich Bonhoeffer, *Ethics,* Macmillan Publishing Company, New York, 1955, p. 58.

[7] Jacqueline Howard, "Americans Devote More Than 10 Hours a Day to Screen Time, and Growing," *CNN,* July 29, 2016, <http://www.cnn.com/2016/06/30/health/americans-screen-time-nielsen/index.html>, accessed on 6/27/17.

[8] Melissa Romero, "How Much Do Americans Really Exercise?" *Washingtonian,* May 10, 2012, <https://www.washingtonian.com/2012/05/10/how-much-do-americans-really-exercise/>, accessed on 6/27/17.

[9] Brady Dennis, "Nearly 60 Percent of Americans—the Highest Ever—Are Taking Prescription Drugs," *The Washington Post,* November 3, 2015, <https://www.washingtonpost.com/news/to-your-health/wp/2015/11/03/more-americans-than-ever-are-taking-prescription-drugs/?utm_term=.4360680550cb>, accessed on 6/27/17.

[10] D.T. Max, "How Humans Are Shaping Our Own Evolution," *National Geographic,* April 2017, <http://www.nationalgeographic.com/magazine/2017/04/evolution-genetics-medicine-brain-technology-cyborg/>, accessed on 6/27/17.

CHAPTER 6

[1] Lisa Eadicicco et al., "The 50 Most Influential Gadgets of All Time," *Time,* May 3, 2016, <http://time.com/4309573/most-influential-gadgets/>, accessed on 6/28/17.

[2] Ingrid Lunden, "80 Percent of All Online Adults Now Own a Smartphone, Less Than 10 Percent Use Wearables," *Techcrunch,* January 12, 2015, <https://techcrunch.com/2015/01/12/80-of-all-online-adults-now-own-a-smartphone-less-than-10-use-wearables/>, accessed 6/29/17.

[3] Webroot, "Internet Pornography by the Numbers; A Significant Threat to Society," <https://www.webroot.com/us/en/home/resources/tips/digital-family-life/internet-pornography-by-the-numbers accessed on 6/29/17.

CHAPTER 7

[1] Ethan Baron, "YouTube Shooter's Father Says She Was Angry at Company," *Mercury News,* April 3, 2018, <https://www.mercurynews.com/2018/04/03/youtube-shooters-father-says-she-was-angry-at-company/>, accessed on 4/4/18.

CHAPTER 8

[1] Kevin Kelly, *What Technology Wants,* Penguin Books, New York, 2010, p. 89.

[2] Thomas L. Friedman, "Is Google God?" *The New York Times,* June 29, 2003, <http://www.nytimes.com/2003/06/29/opinion/is-google-god.html>, accessed on 7/3/17.

[3] Kelly, p. 205.

[4] Rick Paulas, "The Problem with Google's Perceived Omniscience," July 13, 2015, <https://psmag.com/environment/how-google-helps-you-agree-with-yourself>, accessed on 7/4/17.

[5] Andy Crouch, *The Tech-Wise Family,* Baker Books, Grand Rapids, Michigan, 2017, p. 37.

[6] Marshall McLuhan, *Understanding Media,* The MIT Press, Cambridge, Massachusetts, 1964, p. xxi.

CHAPTER 9

[1] Keith, "The History of Social Media: Social Networking Evolution!" *History Cooperative,* <http://historycooperative.org/the-history-of-social-media/>, accessed on 7/5/17.

[2] Mediakix, "How Much Time Do We Spend on Social Media?" <http://mediakix.com/2016/12/how-much-time-is-spent-on-social-media-lifetime/#gs.OjTfzxk>, accessed on 7/5/17.

[3] Sherry Turkle, *Alone Together,* Basic Books, New York, 2011, p 1.

[4] Ibid., p. 15.

[5] Maggie Jackson, *Distracted,* Prometheus Books, Amherst, New York, 2009, p. 14.

[6] Brian A. Primack, MD et al., "Social Media Use and Perceived Social Isolation Among Young Adults in the U.S.," *American Journal of Preventative Medicine,* July 2017, Vol. 53, Issue 1, pp. 1–8, <http://www.ajpmonline.org/article/S0749-3797(17)30016-8/fulltext>, accessed on 7/6/17.

[7] Hanna Krasnova et al., "Envy on Facebook: A Hidden Threat to Users' Life Satisfaction?" <http://www.ara.cat/2013/01/28/855594433.pdf?hash=b775840d43f9f93b7a9031449f809c388f342291>, accessed on 7/6/17.

[8] Shane Hipps, *Flickering Pixels,* Zondervan, Grand Rapids, Michigan, 2009, p. 115.

CHAPTER 10

[1] Marshall McLuhan, *Understanding Media,* MIT Press, Cambridge, Massachusetts, First MIT Edition, 1994, p. 7.

[2] Ferris Jabr, "The Reading Brain in the Digital Age," *Scientific American,* April 11, 2013, <https://www.scientificamerican.com/article/reading-paper-screens/>, accessed on 7/7/17.

[3] Nicholas Carr, "The Web Shatters Focus, Rewires Brains," *Wired,* May 24, 2010, <https://www.wired.com/2010/05/ff_nicholas_carr/>, accessed on 7/7/17.

[4] Nicholas Carr, *The Shallows: What the Internet Is Doing to Our Brains,* W.W. Norton and Company, New York, 2011, p. 90.

[5] Lecia Bushak, "E-Books Are Damaging Your Health: Why We Should All Start Reading Paper Books Again," *Medical Daily,* January 11, 2015, <http://www.medicaldaily.com/e-books-are-damaging-your-health-why-we-should-all-start-reading-paper-books-again-317212>, accessed on 7/7/17.

CHAPTER 11

[1] *Newsweek,* "All Eyes on Google," March 28, 2004, <http://www.newsweek.com/all-eyes-google-124041>, accessed on 7/10/17.

[2] NPR Staff, "The Reason Your Feed Became An Echo Chamber," July 24, 2016, http://www.npr.org/sections/alltechconsidered/2016/07/24/486941582/the-reason-your-feed-became-an-echo-chamber-and-what-to-do-about-it, accessed on 7/10/17.

[3] Lloyd Vries, "Where's Iraq? Young Adults Don't Know," CBS News, June 20, 2007, <http://www.cbsnews.com/news/wheres-iraq-young-adults-dont-know/>, accessed on 7/12/17.

CHAPTER 12

[1] Paul Brand and Philip Yancey, *In His Image,* Zondervan Publishing House, Grand Rapids, Michigan, 1984, p. 121, and Robert L. Martensen, *The Brain Takes Shape,* Oxford University Press, New York, 2004, pp. 49–51.

[2] Jeffrey Schwartz, *The Mind and The Brain,* Regan Books, New York, 2002, p. 175.

[3] Nicholas Carr, *The Shallows: What the Internet Is Doing To Our Brains,* W.W. Norton and Company, New York, 2011, p. 27.

[4] The Conversation, "Outsourcing Memory: The Internet Has Changed How We Remember," November 25, 2012, <http://theconversation.com/outsourcing-memory-the-internet-has-changed-how-we-remember-10871>, accessed on 7/25/17.

CHAPTER 14

[1] Neil Postman, *Amusing Ourselves to Death,* Penguin Books, New York, 1985, p. 161.

[2] The Upfront Analytics Team, "How Marlboro Man Became the First Brand-Repositioning Success Story," June 27, 2016, <http://upfrontanalytics.com/how-marlboro-man-became-the-first-brand-repositioning-success-story/>, accessed on 8/17/17.

[3] Jeanine Poggi, "Flashback Friday: TV's First Commercial Ran 75 Years Ago Today," *AdAge,* July 1, 2016, <http://adage.com/article/media/flash-back-friday-tv-commercial-ran-75-years-ago-today/304777/>, accessed on 11/27/17.

[4] Alec Banks, "The Battle for the Most Expensive Super Bowl Commercial of All Time," Highsnobiety, January 29, 2015, https://www.highsnobiety.com/2015/01/29/most-expensive-super-bowl-commercial/, accessed on 2/12/19.

CHAPTER 15

[1] Sean Goodell, "Cinema as Propaganda During the Third Reich," *Historia: The Alpha Rho Papers,* 2012, p. 144, <epubs.utah.edu/index.php/historia/article/view/627/487>, accessed on 11/29/17.

[2] W. James Potter, *Media Effects,* Sage Publications, Thousand Oaks, California, 2012, pp. 22, 23.

[3] C.S. Lewis, *The Best of C.S. Lewis,* The Iversen Associates, 1969, p. 504.

CHAPTER 16

[1] Oxford Living Dictionaries, <https://en.oxforddictionaries.com/definition/pop_culture>, accessed on 3/19/18.

[2] Alexandre O. Philippe, "Why Pop Culture?" TedxMileHigh, [video clip], <https://www.youtube.com/watch?v=u_3UYncNwz4&vl=en>, accessed on 3/19/18.

[3] Tom Matlack, "Pop Culture Is Killing Us," *The Goodmen Project*, October 17, 2011, <https://goodmenproject.com/featured-content/pop-culture-is-killing-us/>, accessed on 2/12/19.

[4] Neil Postman, *Amusing Ourselves to Death,* Penguin Books, New York, 1985, p. 121.

[5] Dr. Gary Gilley, *This Little Church Went to Market,* Evangelical Press, Darlington, England, 2005, p. 31.

CHAPTER 17

[1] Edwin Sparks, *The Lincoln-Douglas Debates of 1858,* Vol. 1, Springfield, Illinois, Illinois State Historical Library, 1908, p. 4.

[2] Commission on Presidential Debates, <https://www.debates.org/debate-history/2016-debates/>, accessed on 2/12/19.

[3] Linda Rodrigues McRobbie, "The History of Boredom," Smithsonian.com, November 20, 2012, <https://www.smithsonianmag.com/science-nature/the-history-of-boredom-138176427/>, accessed on 12/13/17.

[4] Andy Crouch, *The Tech-Wise Family,* Baker Books, Grand Rapids, Michigan, 2017, p. 145, and *Oxford English Dictionary*, 2nd edition, s.v. "bore."

[5] Sandy Mann, "Why Are We So Bored?" *The Guardian,* April 24, 2016, <https://www.theguardian.com/lifeandstyle/2016/apr/24/why-are-we-so-bored>, accessed on 12/14/17.

[6] Crouch, p. 141.

[7] Chris Weller, "Bill Gates and Steve Jobs Raised Their Kids Tech-Free—And It Should've Been a Red Flag," *Business Insider,* January 10, 2018, <http://www.businessinsider.com/screen-time-limits-bill-gates-steve-jobs-red-flag-2017-10>, accessed on 12/14/17.

[8] Nick Bilton, "Steve Jobs Was a Low-Tech Parent," *The New York Times,* September 10, 2014, <https://www.nytimes.com/2014/09/11/fashion/steve-jobs-apple-was-a-low-tech-parent.html?_r=0>, accessed on 12/14/17.

[9] Mike Allen, "Sean Parker Unloads on Facebook," Axios, November 9, 2017, <https://www.axios.com/sean-parker-unloads-on-facebook-2508036343.html>, accessed on 12/14/17.

CHAPTER 18

[1] Shane Hipps, *Flickering Pixels,* Zondervan, Grand Rapids, Michigan, 2009, pp. 113, 114.

[2] Leah Hickman, "How Social Media Has Become a Sad Substitute for True Community," *Christian Headlines*, March 26, 2018, <https://www.christianheadlines.com/contributors/leah-hickman/how-social-media-has-become-a-sad-substitute-for-true-community.html>, accessed on 3/27/18.

[3] Dena Zaidi, "Meet the Robots Caring for Japan's Aging Population," Venture Beat, November 14, 2017, <https://venturebeat.com/2017/11/14/meet-the-robots-caring-for-japans-aging-population/>, accessed on 12/15/17.

⁴ Peter Feuilherade, "Robots Pick up the Challenge of Home Care Needs," Robohub, April 12, 2017, <http://robohub.org/robots-pick-up-the-challenge-of-home-care-needs/>, accessed on 12/15/17.

Andrew Tarantola, "Robot Caregivers Are Saving the Elderly from Lives of Loneliness," Engadget, August 29, 2017, https://www.engadget.com/2017/08/29/robot-caregivers-are-saving-the-elderly-from-lives-of-loneliness/, accessed on 12/15/17.

Len Calderone, "The New Family Member: A Robotic Caregiver," *Robotics Tomorrow*, December 8, 2015, <https://www.roboticstomorrow.com/article/2015/12/the-new-family-member-a-robotic-caregiver/7312/>, accessed on 12/15/17.

⁵ Sherry Turkle, *Alone Together*, Basic Books, New York, 2011, p. 51.

⁶ Neela Banerjee, "Intimate Confessions Pour Out on Church's Website," *The New York Times*, September 1, 2006, <http://www.nytimes.com/2006/09/01/us/01confession.html?_sm_au_=iHVw1FZBH6wt0vH6>, accessed on 12/15/17.

⁷ N.M. Petry et al., "Internet Gaming Disorder in the DSM-5," National Center for Biotechnology Information, September 2015, <https://www.ncbi.nlm.nih.gov/pubmed/26216590>, accessed on 12/15/17.

⁸ Quoctrung Bui, "Why Some Men Don't Work: Video Games Have Gotten Really Good," *The New York Times*, July 3, 2017, <https://www.nytimes.com/2017/07/03/upshot/why-some-men-dont-work-video-games-have-gotten-really-good.html>, accessed on 12/15/17.

⁹ Kevin Kelly, *What Technology Wants*, Penguin Books, New York, 2010, p. 359.

CHAPTER 19

¹ Laurie Winkless, "Sweating on the Underground," *Forbes*, June 22, 2017, <https://www.forbes.com/sites/lauriewinkless/2017/06/22/sweating-on-the-underground-why-are-tube-tunnels-so-hot/#533ca0745234>, accessed on 12/20/17.

² Rich Sutherland, "25 Facts About the London Underground," Hull Trains, July 22, 2015, <https://www.hulltrains.co.uk/blog/facts/25-facts-about-the-london-underground/#.Wjr6pd-nFhE>, accessed on 12/20/17.

³ Paul Stephen, "Cooling the Tube," *Rail Magazine*, March 2, 2016, <https://www.railmagazine.com/infrastructure/stations/cooling-the-tube>, accessed on 1/9/18.

CHAPTER 22

¹ *A Wake-Up Call*, Ridgeway Books, Medina, New York, 2015, p. 12.

CHAPTER 23

¹ Alexis Kleinman, "Porn Sites Get More Visitors Each Month Than Netflix, Amazon, and Twitter Combined," *The Huffington Post*, <https://www.huffingtonpost.com/2013/05/03/internet-porn-stats_n_3187682.html>, accessed on 12/21/18.

² Andrew Dugan, "More Americans Say Pornography Is Morally Acceptable," Gallup, June 5, 2018, <https://news.gallup.com/poll/235280/americans-say-pornography-morally-acceptable.aspx>, accessed on 12/21/18.

³ CBN News, "Pastors and Porn: The Struggle Is Real," January 29, 2016, <http://www1.cbn.com/cbnnews/us/2016/January/Pastors-and-Porn-The-Struggle-is-Real>, accessed on 2/4/19.

CHAPTER 24

¹ Andy Crouch, *The Tech-Wise Family*, Baker Books, Grand Rapids, Michigan, 2017, p. 186.

CHAPTER 25

¹ Thomas B. Costain, *The Three Edwards*, Doubleday & Company Inc., Garden City, New York, 1958, p. 187.

² Eric Barker, "This Is the Best Way to Overcome Fear of Missing Out," *Time*, June 7, 2016, <http://time.com/4358140/overcome-fomo/>, accessed on 3/7/18.

[3] Aaron Smith, "U.S. Smartphone Use in 2015," Pew Research Center, April 1, 2015, http://www.pewinternet.org/2015/04/01/us-smartphone-use-in-2015/, accessed on 3/8/18.

[4] Katie Reid, "Cutting Connections with Closest Friend: A Smartphone," *Boston Herald,* March 3, 2018, https://newsbout.com/id/18170532129, accessed on 3/7/18.

[5] Oxford Living Dictionaries, <https://en.oxforddictionaries.com/definition/clickbait>, accessed on 3/8/18.

CHAPTER 26

[1] Melany Ethridge, "Digital Bibles Reach Persecuted Church," *Charisma News,* October 6, 2011, <https://www.charismanews.com/culture/32118-digital-bibles-reach-persecuted-church>, accessed on 3/29/18.

[2] *The Voice of the Martyrs,* Bartlesville, Oklahoma, February 2018, pp. 5, 6.

[3] Carey Lodge, "Muslims Converting to Christianity in Saudi Arabia, Despite Intense Persecution," *Christian Today,* May 31, 2016, <https://www.christiantoday.com/article/muslims-converting-to-christianity-in-saudi-arabia-despite-intense-persecution/87220.htm>, accessed on 3/9/18.

[4] Elam, "Elam's Mission," <https://www.elam.com/page/elams-mission>, accessed on 3/29/18.

[5] Stoyan Zaimov, "Iran Spending Millions to Stifle Soaring Christian Population," *The Christian Post,* February 7, 2018, https://www.christianpost.com/news/iran-spending-millions-to-stifle-soaring-christian-population-216770/, accessed on 3/9/18.

[6] David Garrison, *A Wind in the House of Islam,* WIGTake Resources, Monument, Colorado, 2014, Chap. 1.

CHAPTER 27

[1] Antonella Lazarri, "If I Hadn't Spotted That the Sea Was Fizzing . . . ," *The Sun,* December 26, 2014, <https://www.thesun.co.uk/archives/news/635504/if-i-hadnt-spotted-that-the-sea-was-fizzing-then-my-parents-sister-and-me-would-all-be-dead/>, accessed on 3/9/18.

[2] James Owen, "Tsunami Family Saved by Schoolgirl's Geography Lesson," *National Geographic News,* January 18, 2005.

[3] Matt Landis (managing owner, Landis Technologies LLC), personal interview, March 16, 2018.

CHAPTER 28

[1] Tony Reinke, *12 Ways Your Phone Is Changing You,* Crossway, Wheaton, Illinois, 2017, p. 193.

[2] A.W. Tozer, *The Knowledge of the Holy,* Harper Collins Publishers, New York, 1961, p. vii.

[3] Donald S. Whitney, *Spiritual Disciplines for the Christian Life,* NavPress Publishing, Colorado Springs, Colorado, 1991, p. 186.

[4] John Oates, "In Europe You Have Watches, but in Africa We Have Time," *The Register,* January 3, 2005, <https://www.theregister.co.uk/2005/01/03/sahara_crossing/>, accessed on 3/16/18.

ABOUT THE AUTHOR

Gary Miller was raised in California and today lives with his wife Patty and family in the Pacific Northwest. Gary works with the poor in developing countries and directs the SALT Microfinance Solutions program for Christian Aid Ministries. This program offers business and spiritual teaching to those living in chronic poverty, provides small loans, sets up local village savings groups, and assists them in learning how to use their God-given resources to become sustainable.

Gary has authored the Kingdom-Focused Living Series, microfinance manuals, and several booklets for outreach purposes. For a list of his books and other resource materials, see page 231.

Have you been inspired by Gary's materials? Maybe you have questions, or perhaps you even disagree with the author. Share your thoughts by sending an e-mail to kingdomfinance@camoh.org or writing to Christian Aid Ministries, P.O. Box 360, Berlin, Ohio 44610.

ADDITIONAL RESOURCES BY GARY MILLER

BOOKS

Kingdom-Focused Finances for the Family
This first book in the Kingdom-Focused Living series is realistic, humorous, and serious about getting us to become stewards instead of owners.

Charting a Course in Your Youth
A serious call to youth to examine their faith, focus, and finances. Second book in Kingdom-Focused Living series.

Going Till You're Gone
A plea for godly examples—for older men and women who will demonstrate a kingdom-focused vision all the way to the finish line. Third book in Kingdom-Focused Living series.

The Other Side of the Wall
Stresses Biblical principles that apply to all Christians who want to reflect God's heart in giving. Applying these principles has the potential to change lives—first our own, and then the people God calls us to share with. Fourth book in Kingdom-Focused Living series.

It's Not Your Business

How involved in business should followers of Jesus be? Did God intend the workplace to play a prominent role in building his kingdom? Explore the benefits and dangers in business. Fifth and final book in the Kingdom-Focused Living series.

Budgeting Made Simple

A budgeting workbook in a ring binder; complements *Kingdom-Focused Finances for the Family*.

What Happened to Our Money?

Ignorance of Biblical money management can set young people on a path of financial hardship that results in anxiety, marital discord, depression, and envy. This short book presents foundational truths on which young couples can build their financial lives.

Life in a Global Village

Would your worldview change if the world population were shrunk to a village of one hundred people and you lived in that village? Full-color book.

This Side of the Global Wall

Pictures and graphs in this full-color book portray the unprecedented opportunities Americans have today. What are we doing with the resources God has given us?

Small Business Handbook

A manual used in microfinance programs in developing countries. Includes devotionals and practical business teaching. Ideal for missions and churches.

Following Jesus in Everyday Life

A teaching manual ideal for mission settings. Each lesson addresses a Biblical principle and includes a story and discussion questions. Black and white illustrations.

A Good Soldier of Jesus Christ

A teaching manual like *Following Jesus in Everyday Life*, but targeting youth.

Know Before You Go

Every year, thousands of Americans travel to distant countries to help the needy. But could some of these short-term mission trips be doing more harm than good? This book encourages us to reexamine our goals and methods, and prepares people to effectively interact with other cultures in short-term missions.

Jesus Really Said That?

This book presents five teachings of Jesus that are often missed, ignored, or rejected. It tells the story of Jeremy and Alicia, a couple who thought they understood Christianity and knew what it meant to be a Christian . . . until they began to look at what Jesus actually said!

Radical Islam

From the barbarous actions of ISIS to the shocking tactics of Al-Qaida, radical Islamic extremists seem to be everywhere and growing stronger. Many wonder in alarm if the movement will overtake the West and change Americans' way of life forever. How should Christians respond to this threat? Does the Bible have answers? How would Jesus respond?

How Can Anyone Say God Is Good?

Nick is fed up with life and aggravated by the simple-minded people who believe in a supreme being in spite of all the agony and chaos around them. How can they have the audacity to say their God is good? Written in story form and ending with the author's personal journey, this book is a good gift for an agnostic or atheist friend. It can also be used to strengthen the faith of a Christian believer.

Church Matters

How can we increase the impact of our churches on the world around us? Why do we struggle to be a light to the world? Are splits and disagreements okay? Compare the current state of the church with God's original vision in the book of Acts. This book will challenge your Christian life and possibly your ideology of the church.

SEMINARS

Kingdom-Focused Finances—Audio

This three-session seminar takes you beyond our culture's view of money and possessions, and challenges you to examine your heart by looking at your treasure. Three CDs.

Kingdom-Focused Finances—Audio and Visual

Follow along on the slides Gary uses in his seminars while you listen to the presentation. A good tool for group study or individual use. A computer is needed to view these three CDs.

AUDIO BOOKS

Kingdom-Focused Finances for the Family
Charting a Course in Your Youth
Going Till You're Gone
The Other Side of the Wall
It's Not Your Business
Life in a Global Village
Church Matters
Surviving the Tech Tsunami

BIBLIOGRAPHY

Bennetch, Luke, *The Pilgrim and Technology*, Christian Light Publications, Harrisonburg, Virginia, 2013.

Berry, Wendell, *The Gift of the Good Land*, North Point Press, San Francisco, 1982.

Bonhoeffer, Dietrich, *Ethics*, Macmillan Publishing Company, New York, 1955.

Carr, Nicholas, *The Shallows: What the Internet Is Doing to Our Brains*, W.W. Norton and Company, New York, 2011.

Crouch, Andy, *The Tech-Wise Family*, Baker Books, Grand Rapids, Michigan, 2017.

Ellul, Jacques, *The Technological Society*, Vintage Books, New York, 1964.

Garrison, David, *A Wind in the House of Islam*, WIGTake Resources, Monument, Colorado, 2014.

Gilley, Dr. Gary, *This Little Church Went to Market*, Evangelical Press, Darlington, England, 2005.

Gleick, James, *Faster—The Acceleration of Just About Everything*, Vintage Books, New York, 1999.

Hipps, Shane, *Flickering Pixels*, Zondervan, Grand Rapids, Michigan, 2009.

———, *The Hidden Power of Electronic Culture*, Zondervan, Grand Rapids, Michigan, 2005.

Jackson, Maggie, *Distracted*, Prometheus Books, New York, 2009.

Kandel, Eric, *In Search of Memory*, W.W. Norton and Company, London, 2006.

Kelly, Kevin, *What Technology Wants*, Penguin Books, New York, 2010.

Lanier, Jaron, *You Are Not a Gadget*, Thorndike Press, Waterville, Maine, 2010.

McLuhan, Marshall, *Understanding Media*, The MIT Press, Cambridge, Massachusetts, 1964.

Postman, Neil, *Amusing Ourselves to Death*, Penguin Books, New York, 1985.

———, *Technopoly—The Surrender of Culture to Technology*, Random House, New York, 1992.

Potter, W. James, *Media Effects*, Sage Publications, Thousand Oaks, California, 2012.

Reinke, Tony, *12 Ways Your Phone Is Changing You*, Crossway, Wheaton, Illinois, 2017.

Tozer, A.W., *Worship and Entertainment*, WingSpread Publishers, Camp Hill, Pennsylvania, 1997.

Turkle, Sherry, *Alone Together*, Basic Books, New York, 2011.

Walsh, Anthony and Jonathan Bolen, *The Neurobiology of Human Behavior*, Routledge Publishers, London, 2016.

Warren, Michael, *Seeing Through the Media*, Trinity Press International, Harrisburg, Pennsylvania, 1997.

Whitney, Donald, *Spiritual Disciplines for the Christian Life*, NavPress, Colorado Springs, Colorado, 1991.

ABOUT CHRISTIAN AID MINISTRIES

Christian Aid Ministries was founded in 1981 as a nonprofit, tax-exempt 501(c)(3) organization. Its primary purpose is to provide a trustworthy and efficient channel for Amish, Mennonite, and other conservative Anabaptist groups and individuals to minister to physical and spiritual needs around the world. This is in response to the command to ". . . do good unto all men, especially unto them who are of the household of faith" (Galatians 6:10).

Each year, CAM supporters provide 15–20 million pounds of food, clothing, medicines, seeds, Bibles, Bible story books, and other Christian literature for needy people. Most of the aid goes to orphans and Christian families. Supporters' funds also help to clean up and rebuild for natural disaster victims, put up Gospel billboards in the U.S., support several church-planting efforts, operate two medical clinics, and provide resources for needy families to make their own living. CAM's main purposes for providing aid are to help and encourage God's people and bring the Gospel to a lost and dying world.

CAM has staff, warehouses, and distribution networks in Romania, Moldova, Ukraine, Haiti, Nicaragua, Liberia, Israel, and

Kenya. Aside from management, supervisory personnel, and bookkeeping operations, volunteers do most of the work at CAM locations. Each year, volunteers at our warehouses, field bases, Disaster Response Services projects, and other locations donate over 200,000 hours of work.

CAM's ultimate purpose is to glorify God and help enlarge His kingdom. ". . . whatsoever ye do, do all to the glory of God" (1 Corinthians 10:31).

THE WAY TO GOD AND PEACE

We live in a world contaminated by sin. Sin is anything that goes against God's holy standards. When we do not follow the guidelines that God our Creator gave us, we are guilty of sin. Sin separates us from God, the source of life.

Since the time when the first man and woman, Adam and Eve, sinned in the Garden of Eden, sin has been universal. The Bible says that we all have "sinned and come short of the glory of God" (Romans 3:23). It also says that the natural consequence for that sin is eternal death, or punishment in an eternal hell: "Then when lust hath conceived, it bringeth forth sin: and sin, when it is finished, bringeth forth death" (James 1:15).

But we do not have to suffer eternal death in hell. God provided forgiveness for our sins through the death of His only Son, Jesus Christ. Because Jesus was perfect and without sin, He could die in our place. "For God so loved the world that he gave his only begotten Son, that whosoever believeth in him should not perish, but have everlasting life" (John 3:16).

A sacrifice is something given to benefit someone else. It costs the giver greatly. Jesus was God's sacrifice. Jesus' death takes away the penalty of sin for all those who accept this sacrifice and truly repent of their sins. To repent of sins means to be truly sorry for and turn away from the things we have done that have violated God's standards (Acts 2:38; 3:19).

Jesus died, but He did not remain dead. After three days, God's Spirit miraculously raised Him to life again. God's Spirit does something similar in us. When we receive Jesus as our sacrifice and repent of our sins, our hearts are changed. We become spiritually alive! We develop new desires and attitudes (2 Corinthians 5:17). We begin to make choices that please God (1 John 3:9). If we do fail and commit sins, we can ask God for forgiveness. "If we confess our sins, he is faithful and just to forgive us our sins, and to cleanse us from all unrighteousness" (1 John 1:9).

Once our hearts have been changed, we want to continue growing spiritually. We will be happy to let Jesus be the Master of our lives and will want to become more like Him. To do this, we must meditate on God's Word and commune with God in prayer. We will testify to others of this change by being baptized and sharing the good news of God's victory over sin and death. Fellowship with a faithful group of believers will strengthen our walk with God (1 John 1:7).